THE
LANDS
NO ONE
KNOWS

THE LANDS NO ONE KNOWS

America and the Public Domain

**T. H. WATKINS and
CHARLES S. WATSON, JR.**

SIERRA CLUB BOOKS • SAN FRANCISCO • 1975

The Sierra Club, founded in 1892 by John Muir, has
devoted itself to the study and protection of the nation's
scenic and ecological resources—mountains, wetlands,
woodlands, wild shores and rivers. All club publications
are part of the nonprofit effort the Club carries on as a
public trust. There are over 50 chapters coast to coast, in
Canada, Hawaii and Alaska. Participation is invited in
the Club's program to enjoy and preserve wilderness
everywhere. Address: 1050 Mills Tower, San Francisco,
California 94104.

The quotation on page 54 is from *Beyond the Hundredth
Meridian: John Wesley Powell and the Second Opening
of the West*, by Wallace Stegner. Copyright © 1954 by
Wallace E. Stegner. Reprinted by permission of Houghton
Mifflin Co., Boston.

The quotation on page 124 is from *The Easy Chair* by
Bernard DeVoto. Copyright © 1955 by Bernard DeVoto.
Reprinted by permission of Helen Avis DeVoto and
Houghton Mifflin Co., Boston.

Library of Congress Cataloging in Publication Data

Watkins, T. H.
  The lands no one knows.

  Includes index.
  1. United States—Public lands. 2. Environmental policy—
United States. I. Watson, Charles S., 1932–   joint author.
II. Title.
KF5605.W35   346'.73'044   75-1276
ISBN 0-87156-130-1

Design by John Beyer
Production by David Charlsen/Charlsen + Johansen & Others.
PRINTED IN THE UNITED STATES OF AMERICA.

This book is dedicated to the memory of

GEORGE KELL
1905–1968

Friend, defender, and advocate for the American land

"We are waking now from the American dream to realize that it was a dream few Americans lived in their waking hours. The history of the New World has turned out to be not so different from that of the Old. The peril that threatens the last of the American wilderness arises not from the reckless dream, but from the same historic forces of rapacity and cruelty that laid waste the land in the Mediterranean Basin, in Arabia, India, and the treeless uplands of China."

GERARD PIEL

CONTENTS

PREFACE

WHAT FOLLOWS is the story of a squandered inheritance, an inheritance vouchsafed the citizens of this country nearly two hundred years ago: the public domain, a theory that became fact by proclamation of the Continental Congress in 1779. Next to the Constitution and the Bill of Rights, it was probably the single most important development to emerge from the rancorous years of national organization that accompanied and followed the Revolutionary War. Like those two venerable legacies, the public domain has been harried by generations of misinterpretation, confusion, subversion, and abuse. Unlike them, much of the public domain did not survive. We are the poorer for that fact.

The public domain was land, held in trust by the federal government and owned by the people of the United States—all of the people of the United States. At its greatest, this patrimony of land included 2.1 billion acres in the continental United States and territories and Alaska, together with all the mountain ranges, hills, forests, woods, meadows, rivers, lakes, ponds, estuaries, grazing and agricultural lands, and deserts appertaining thereto—all of this ideally to "be disposed of for the common benefit of the United States." Over the past 194 years, more than half of this national inheritance has indeed been "disposed of" in one manner or another, but to whose "benefit" is a question still rattling around in the coffin of history. Most of it was simply given away in chunks and dribbles—by grants to states and railroad corporations, by direct sales at bargain rates to mining, farming, ranching, and timber interests and to land jobbers who reaped spectacular profits with the connivance of local, state, and federal officials, by legitimate land laws whose rules and spirit were honored more often in the breach than in the observance, and by illegitimate land laws whose only visible purpose was to carve out pieces of federal land for the enrichment of a few.

Today, the federal government owns and administers approximately 765 million acres of public lands; 312 million acres are

*Inheritance: A granite peak rises like a fist above a
snow-covered meadow in the San Miguel Mountains of Colorado.*

under the control of the National Park Service, Forest Service, Bureau of Indian Affairs, Bureau of Sport Fisheries and Wildlife, Bureau of Reclamation, Department of Defense, Department of State, Atomic Energy Commission, Tennessee Valley Authority, and the National Aeronautics and Space Administration. The remaining 453 million acres, aptly dubbed the "National Resource Lands" in federalese, are administered by the Bureau of Land Management and comprise the present public domain. The largest portion of this land—nearly 300 million acres—is in Alaska, but it also makes up some two-thirds of the state of Nevada, half or more of Utah, nearly half of New Mexico and Wyoming, and significant portions of California, Idaho, Arizona, Oregon, Colorado, and Montana, as well as smaller parts of many eastern states. In acreage alone, the remaining public domain obviously is one of the nation's most valuable assets, yet it continues to be victimized by ignorance, neglect, conflicting uses, contradictory regulations, and confused and confusing management practices.

In the past, even in the pit of what historian Vernon L. Parrington called "The Great Barbecue" of the nineteenth century, the public domain had its champions in and out of government. Among them were Major John Wesley Powell, whose *Report on the Lands of the Arid Region of the United States* in 1878 advocated the division of the West along geographic rather than political lines and a rational use of the land's resources; Land Commissioner William Andrew Jackson Sparks, whose attempt to protect the public domain from the sundry agents of plunder caused his dismissal in 1887; Gifford Pinchot, a public servant whose advocacy helped create those public domain reserves that later became our National Forest system; Representative Edward I. Taylor of Colorado, author of the Taylor Grazing Act of 1934; and closer to our own time, Bernard DeVoto, who in the years following World War II leveled the howitzer of his splendid prose in the pages of *Harper's* magazine to help stifle the attempt of those whom he called "Two-Gun Desmonds" to wrest the national lands from the federal government and place them in the control of the individual states. To the efforts of such men—and there were many more—we owe the very existence of that part of the original public domain that has survived the generations. But there are generations to come, and if we hope to bequeath this legacy intact, we will need the insight, determination, and strength of similar men.

Which brings us to the point of this preface. Although the text for *The Lands No One Knows* was written by myself, the name of Charles S. Watson, Jr. appears on the book as co-author for good and sufficient reasons. Watson would be the last man in the world to compare himself to Major Powell, or even William Andrew Jackson Sparks, nor would he willingly maintain that he has stood alone against those who would dismember the public domain. Yet the fact remains that for more than twenty years he has been profoundly involved with these lands—as an amateur explorer with a professional's knowledge of geology and cartography, as an advocate of reform with a zealot's persistence and a lobbyist's comprehension of the intricacies of the governmental labyrinth, as a stand-up, out-front public spokesman with an athlete's disregard of verbal abuse and physical threats, of which he has enjoyed more than his share. Short, bald, blue-eyed, and built like a Sherman tank, he is a formidable opponent and an intensely informed representative of lands that cannot speak for themselves.

Born in Ohio and reared in southern California, Watson's love affair with the public domain began as a high school student with field trips into the wilderness of the Mojave Desert, continued during his studies at the University of Nevada's Mackay School of Mines in Reno, Nevada, and was first expressed in 1958, when with a handful of like-minded persons he organized the Nevada Public Domain Survey, whose goal was nothing less than a quadrant-by-quadrant examination of the 48.9 million acres of Bureau of Land Management territory in Nevada, seeking out those pockets and stretches that should be preserved as wilderness or utilized for recreation. The survey launched, Watson entered government service in 1960, first with the Bureau of Land Management in Reno, then with the Naval Oceanographic Office in Washington, D.C., and finally with the Aeronautical Chart and Information Service of the Air Force in St. Louis. He departed the government in 1972 to continue his conservation activities, which had increased during those twelve years, often to the point of open conflict with his superiors, who were no more enthusiastic than such officials usually are at the prospect of a federal employee capable of independent opinion (not to mention action).

In 1965 the little group of public-domain enthusiasts was reorganized into the Nevada Outdoor Recreation Association (NORA), and Watson assembled a separate, though related, organization —the National Public Lands Task Force—as a political and propaganda force. In that same year, he presented an illustrated lecture in Washington that was attended by Mrs. Lyndon B. Johnson and members of the staff of Secretary of the Interior Stewart Udall, among others—including Bureau of Land Management chief, Eldon F. Holmes—and spent weeks carrying around the Nevada

Survey, which by then included 450 site discoveries and weighed approximately twenty-five pounds, to demonstrate to members of Congress and officials in the Bureau of Land Management and the National Park Service that the public domain was a cornucopia of such wilderness treasures as Leviathan Cave, Blue Lake, Red Rock Canyon, the Goblin Garden, High Rock Canyon, and scores of equally splendid sites—all of these in Nevada alone. He may have started no fires, but sparks were struck; the National Park Service later described the survey as a "monumental achievement in the identification of a state's public land resources," and it was no coincidence, one suspects, that in 1968 the Bureau of Land Management issued its own illustrated guide listing 432 points of interest on the lands it administers (Eldon F. Holmes had been more than a little impressed by Watson's 1965 presentation).

Today, NORA and its political arm, the National Public Lands Task Force, number more than 700 members in seventeen states —no monolith, but an organization whose singleness of purpose has given it an influence beyond numbers and gained it the support of such relatively powerful allies as the Sierra Club, the National Resources Defense Council, the Trust for Public Land, Friends of the Earth, the Wilderness Society, The Nature Conservancy, and Stewart Brand's "POINT" organization. The original survey is expanding to someday include every state that contains public-domain lands. As Director and Representative-at-Large of the Task Force, Watson continues to promote the activities of the movement that is his child and his love, moving about the deserts and mountains in his miniature cab-over Datsun camper, maintaining a blinding stream of correspondence with congressmen and senators, conservationists and real estate promoters, bureau chiefs and division heads, strangers and friends, badgering Bureau of Land Management officials and testifying at the drop of a gavel, constantly adding to public-domain files that already must be thirty feet deep (surely the most comprehensive such archive outside the Washington headquarters of the Bureau of Land Management), painstakingly keeping up the massive scrapbooks that document the discoveries of his NORA compatriots, holding press conferences whenever he can find a reporter willing to listen, issuing a monthly newsletter, and writing hardnosed polemics for such publications as the Sierra Club *Bulletin* and *National Parks Magazine*.

It is reliably reported that he has been known to sleep, and I can personally testify that he eats, since I once shared a pot of his powerful chili. Still, Watson's life is quite literally his work. Like other men with such a clarity of purpose, he has been called obsessed; for myself, I will call him dedicated in the truest, most selfless sense of the word, dedicated to the proposition that the public domain is not some vague wasteland to be ignored or gotten rid of, but a precious national resource, the largest part of what we have left to give to those who must follow us. To him, it is our inheritance and our trust, and to lose it to the ripoff artists of the world —as so much if it has already been lost—would be to lose a good part of what America means. Grown men have spent their lives pursuing less admirable convictions.

"Such is oft the course of deeds that move the wheels of the world," J. R. R. Tolkien wrote. "Small hands do them because they must, while the eyes of the great are elsewhere." It is of the efforts of such men as Charles S. Watson, Jr. that reforms are made, and it is of the dreams of such men that books like this are made. *The Lands No One Knows* was his conception, a vision translated here into another man's language. The twenty years of his research lie at its heart, and since no one knows more of what has happened, is happening, and is likely to happen to the public domain, his thoughts and perceptions have guided its writing from beginning to end. *The Lands No One Knows*, then, is a genuine collaboration: if the words of the book are mine, its meaning and its purpose belong to him. *Salud*, Charlie.

T. H. WATKINS
San Francisco
December 1974

PART ONE:

THE INHERITANCE

*"This noblest patrimony ever
yet inherited by any people must
be husbanded and preserved with
care, in such manner that future
generations shall not reproach
us with having squandered what
was justly theirs. . . . "*

—THE WHIG ALMANAC, 1843

Older than the human dream of land, older than the land speculations of George Washington, older than the very concept of the public domain, a bristlecone pine documents time in the White Mountains of California.

I
PERPLEXITIES AND PROFIT

THE DREAM BEGAN WITH LAND. Like the answer to the prayers of human opportunity, the American continent stretched west until it lost itself beyond the horizon. No one knew how far it went or how rich it was. But it was enough, and more than enough. Beginning with the Royal English Charter of 1605, which granted the Virginia Company the power to "make habitation, plantation, and to deduce a colony of sundry of our people into 'that part of America commonly called Virginia," six colonial grants had stipulated northern and southern boundaries that swept quite literally from sea to shining sea. Each of the fortunate six (Massachusetts, Connecticut, North Carolina, South Carolina, Georgia, and Virginia) thus acquired, on paper, a three-thousand-mile strip of the American continent.

Virginia, in fact, claimed even more than that, since her charter sent her boundaries "up into the land, throughout from sea to sea, west and northwest," giving her effective control of what would become Kentucky and nearly all lands north and west of the Ohio River. New York, to make things interesting, also claimed much of this land, on the grounds that her jurisdiction over the expansion-minded Iroquois Indians applied to all lands that tribe controlled through the rigorous application of the tomahawk. By the time of the American Revolution, the inconvenience of Spanish possession of the western two-thirds of the continent had chopped these grandiose claims clear back to the Mississippi River, but they still included millions upon millions of acres, an immense colonial patrimony of crowded timberlands, navigable rivers, and most importantly, bottomlands whose soil was so rich and moist that a man could mold it in his fist.

That land was more than a temptation; it was the visible gratification of generations of hunger, a hunger carried to the New

19

World as part of the mental baggage of the first seasick voyagers who stumbled ashore at Jamestown, Virginia in 1607, as well as those who followed them. Land was opportunity. Land was wealth. Land was power. Land was even a kind of nobility. These certainties, as much a part of the makeup of the English settlers of America as the genes that determined the color of their eyes, were sharpened by the colonial experience. Hampered by severe restrictions on industry and commerce, those who were driven, as Francis Parkman put it, "by an insane desire to better their condition in life" had only land to satisfy the compulsion. It was the headright grants, ranging in size from 20 to 100 acres, that inspired those yeomen who could afford the passage to emigrate to the colonies. It was New England's military land grants that encouraged such transplanted yeomen to enlist in the various colonial wars. And it was the unsurveyed and unappropriated lands of the trans-Appalachian West that called such men across the mountains and fueled dreams of empire and avarice in the minds of those who were higher on the economic scale.

The urge for land was a powerful, and to the authorities in England, a worrisome thing. In 1763, when the conclusion of the Seven Years' War gave England uncontested control of all territory east of the Mississippi River, those authorities rescinded the original colonial land grants and prohibited settlement or land acquisitions west of the Appalachian Mountains, on the contention that encroachment on the Indian lands would not only result in violence but, more importantly, disrupt the lucrative fur trade. As might be expected, this Proclamation of 1763, as unrealistic as it was unenforceable, was largely ignored by the colonials.

A case in point is the example of George Washington of Mount Vernon, Virginia. Washington, who had distinguished himself as a gentleman-soldier during the Seven Years' War, had larger ambitions; namely, he wanted to become a gentleman-landlord of spectacular dimensions and was not about to let an order he dismissed as "a scrap of paper" stand in his way. Writing to his friend and agent, Captain William Crawford, in 1763, Washington noted: "I offered in my last to join you in attempting to secure some of the most valuable lands in the King's part, which I think may be accomplished after awhile, notwithstanding the proclamation that restrains it at present and prohibits the settlement of them at all; for I can never look upon that proclamation in any other light (but this I say between ourselves) than as a temporary expedient to quiet the minds of the Indians. It must fall, of course, in a few years. . . . Any person, therefore who neglects the present opportunity of hunting out good lands, and in some measure marking and distinguishing them for his own, in order to keep others from settling them, will never regain it." It took him ten years of investigation and cautious maneuvering, but in 1773 Washington felt confident enough to advertise his possession of 20,000 acres on the banks of the Ohio and Great Kanawha rivers, which he proposed to divide "into any sized tenements that may be desired, and lease them upon moderate terms. . . ."

Washington was hardly alone in such enterprises. Scores of men who in a few years would form the leadership of the new Republic—among them Benjamin Franklin, George Clinton, Patrick Henry, and Gouverneur Morris—threw their energies into the purchase of western lands. Some, like Washington, hoped to retain the land as a kind of permanent barony, but most were interested in it as a speculation, to be bought cheaply and sold as high as the traffic would bear. (Even Washington ultimately abandoned landlordism; writing in 1794, he lamented that "I have found distant property in land more pregnant of perplexities than profit. I have therefore resolved to sell all I hold on the western waters, if I can obtain the prices which I conceive their quality, their situation, and other advantages would authorize me to expect.") Possessed by the speculator's itch and inflamed expectations, they formed such purchasing and marketing organizations as the Ohio Company, Illinois Company, Indiana Company, Mississippi Company, Transylvania Company (truly), Wabash Company, and the Vandalia Company, laid claim to millions of acres of western lands, and eagerly awaited the inevitable boom.

None of these inflated schemes survived the Revolution. They were, in fact, crippled the very moment the individual colonies made the painful decision to coalesce into "a more perfect union," for one of the most important matters to be resolved before any such union, perfect or no, could be established was the disposition of the western lands that would be reacquired upon victory over England. As the sentiment for organization grew during the 1770s, so did the conviction that the western land claims of individual colonies should be turned over to the union as the price of admission. This point of view, unsurprisingly, was most vigorously put forward by the landless colonies (Maryland, Rhode Island, New Hampshire, New Jersey, Pennsylvania, and Delaware). Among other things, these colonies feared that local taxes, their principal means of raising money, would drive citizens away to the landed colonies, which could depend upon land sales for the bulk of their financing if they were allowed to keep their trans-Appalachian

OVERLEAF: Part of the settlers' inheritance—the Presidential Range of New Hampshire, looking west, always west.

claims. After the beginning of the war with England, the opinions of the landless colonies were echoed by the Continental Congress, for equally unsurprising reasons: land was money, and the embryonic government of the not-yet United States was in desperate need of revenue and knew that this need would continue indefinitely. A final—and significant—measure of support came from ever-present land speculators, who viewed the national ownership of these lands as a rich pie, ready for carving. Inasmuch as many of these same speculators were members, relatives of members, friends of members, or friends of relatives of members of the government itself, it was not a farfetched notion.

The landed colonies, which had money problems and hungry speculators of their own to contend with, resisted the whole idea, but in vain. Even though they outnumbered the landless colonies (if we include New York's somewhat vague claims to the lands under the sway of the Iroquois), the pressures were enormous and telling. In 1778, Maryland, the leading opponent of the landed colonies, announced that it would not ratify the pending Articles of Confederation unless each colony-about-to-become-state granted whatever western lands it might hold to the central government. Maryland claimed to be acting out of concern for the larger good of the country, since it had no visible special interest in the disposal of western lands (although the speculators who infested its government like carpenter ants certainly did). Those states whose interest was visible indeed found it more difficult to hide behind pretty rhetoric, for if they refused to accede to Maryland's demands, they were patently willing to axe the creation of a viable national government for no better motive than simple greed. Virginia, which had claim to more land than any other colony, was particularly distressed by the situation, for the members of its government knew perfectly well what dreams fermented in the brains of Maryland's small army of speculators, as well as those of other landless colonies.

The problem for the landed colonies was compounded immeasurably on October 30, 1779, when the Continental Congress formally requested the transfer of western lands, and was further complicated on October 10, 1780, when Congress repeated the request and stated the hallowed concept of the public domain as it would come to be understood: "*Resolved*, that the unappropriated lands that may be ceded or relinquished to the United States, by any particular States, pursuant to the recommendation of Congress . . . shall be disposed of for the common benefit of the United States, and be settled and formed into distinct republican

A glacial cirque on Mount Katahdin, the highest mountain peak found in Maine and one of the earliest wilderness legacies of a young America.

States, which shall become members of the Federal Union, and shall have the same rights of sovereignty, freedom, and independence, as the other states. . . ." This resolution was too much —certainly for New York, which almost immediately ceded its highly dubious claim to Iroquois lands. It was even too much for Virginia, which had the most to lose. In making its cession in 1780, however, the state imposed one canny stipulation—that the legislature would consider the transfer legal only if Congress invalidated all previous or current private purchases in the region involved, thus eliminating *all* speculative claims, at least temporarily. If that could be agreed upon, the state would give up its lands "in full confidence that Congress will in justice to this State for the liberal Cession she hath made earnestly press upon the other States claiming large Tracts of waste and uncultivated Territory the propriety of making Cessions equally liberal for the common Benefit and support of the Union." Those speculators in and out of Virginia who had invested time and money in the lands in question of course set up a piteous howl in the halls of Congress, but after nearly four years of bickering, the government of the United States accepted Virginia's cession with the stipulation intact. One by one, the other landed colonies relinquished their claims. Except for a number of "reserves" held back by several states to satisfy land bounties given to members of local militia for their services during the Revolution, by 1802 the United States had become the owner and administrator of the ancestral public domain, nearly 300 million acres of land between the Appalachian Mountains and the Mississippi River.

Shortly after the Virginia cession was accepted, Congress passed the first national land law in American history. Unlike most of the thousands that would follow it over the next century-and-a-half, it was not only an example of plain common sense, but an utterly sincere effort to solve a national problem on a national scale and in the national interest. This was the Ordinance of 1785, which historian Payson J. Treat called "one of the wisest and most influential of all the acts of the Revolutionary period." Under its provisions, the newly established public domain was to be surveyed and divided into townships six miles to a side. These, in turn, would be subdivided into thirty-six numbered sections of one square mile each (640 acres). After the first range of seven townships in any given region was surveyed, whole townships as well as individual sections would be offered for sale at public auctions to be held in each of the original thirteen states; purchases of less than 640 acres would be barred, and the minimum bid allowed would be $640. Congress reserved to itself sections 8, 11, 26, and 29 in each township, as well as one-third of all gold, silver, lead, and copper mines that might be discovered therein, and section 16 was to be set aside for the support of public schools.

A pragmatic reaction to nearly two centuries of British land policy—which had made up in confusion what it had lacked in consistency—the Ordinance of 1785 was unquestionably influential, as Payson noted; ultimately, almost every civilized nation in the world adopted its system of surveys. Yet not even this careful, sincerely conceived legislation would prove to be adequate to protect the national lands from systematic abuse, for they were trapped in the passion of centuries. Land was still money, and for so long as it was looked upon basically as a commodity to be gotten rid of rather than a resource to be managed, history would assure its victimization by chicanery, jobbery, and monopoly, no matter what laws might be worked out to govern its disposal. In practice, if not in theory, land laws were made to be circumvented, and almost from the date of its birth, the American public domain entered its decline.

Sun City, Arizona, the lineal descendent of the real
estate dreams of George Washington and his colleagues.

II
SO SUBLIME
IN PRINCIPLE

IN 1842, an otherwise obscure Missouri congressman rose to his feet in the Capitol in Washington, D.C. and gave definition to the instincts of an age: "There is such a thing," he said, "as a destiny for this American race ... because we, the people of the United States, have spread, are spreading, and intend to spread, and should spread, and go on to spread ... and this our destiny has now become so manifest that it cannot fail but by our own folly."

Destiny made manifest: in 1803 the Louisiana Territory was purchased from France, which at a cost of approximately 3.6 cents an acre made this, in the words of one historian, "one of the greatest bargains ever struck off by the hand of man." In 1819 Florida was purchased from Spain; in 1845 the Republic of Texas became the state of Texas by virtue of annexation to the United States; in 1846 the Oregon Territory was acquired from Great Britain by treaty; in 1848 the conclusion of the Mexican War brought the Mexican Cession, including all of California, Nevada, and New Mexico, most of Arizona, and parts of Colorado and Utah; in 1853 the Gadsden Purchase finished off the Arizona acquisition; and in 1867 the purchase of Alaska from Russia added a final sweep of territory to the country. In a little over three generations the boundaries and people of the United States had indeed gone on to spread, and in the process the federal government had become the proprietor of 1,817,572,200 acres of land in addition to the 300 million acres of the original public domain.[1]

The disposition of this immense patrimony of land was from the beginning tangled in a welter of emotional, economic, and entrepreneurial considerations that simply obliterated any possibility that it could be accomplished within hailing distance of logic or consistency. Reason was lost in a swamp of pragmatism and inarguable ideals—as well as some rather cottony rhetoric. "No

29

America would spread, and did spread, until all the westward-leading tracks met the waves of the Pacific.

other country or age," the editor of the *National Intelligencer* wrote in 1819, "has produced a land system so sublime in principle, so perfect in practice, so magnificent in prospect.... Greece in its wisdom, Rome in its grandeur, Europe in its glory, never realized a system so deserving the admiration and applause of human-kind." After all, who could reasonably maintain that there·was something wrong, in theory, with the idea that the federal government should sell land as one means of supporting itself; that it should aid the financing of local education through land grants; that it should compensate American Indians for reservation lands confiscated during the period of Indian concentration following the Civil War, either by allowing the Indians to sell their reservation lands directly or through the government; that it should encourage the reclamation of arable lands by making grants of "swamp" and "overflow" lands to the states; that it should use federal lands to help finance the construction of vital public improvements, such as canals and railroads, giving private capital the incentive to invest in such works; and finally, that it should make land available to genuine settlers and farmers at the cheapest, most convenient rates possible as a means of encouraging settlement and development? Such were the principles involved, and if not exactly sublime, they were inarguably well-intentioned. Like Jacob wrestling with his angel, the federal government struggled manfully for more than a century to implement them. And while it struggled, the land slipped away.

As noted in Chapter 1, the Ordinance of 1785 was designed to assure the orderly disposal of the original public domain. A related measure, the Ordinance of 1787, was an equally pragmatic device that provided for the gradual assimilation of these lands into the Union as political entities, first as territories when a population of five thousand or more had settled a given region and its citizens had banded together to elect territorial representatives, then as states when the population had grown to fifty thousand or more, its citizens had voted for statehood, and a petition for such status had been presented to and approved by Congress. With minor revisions, the Ordinance of 1787 continued to function well into the twentieth century. Not as much can be said for the Ordinance of 1785, which was immediately beset by sharp-eyed speculators only too willing to exploit its weaknesses and by a westward-inclining population that voiced increasingly powerful demands to liberalize the land-sale provisions.

In the years immediately after the end of the Revolution the eastern seaboard was a stewpot of speculation in state lands and military bounty lands; by 1792, for example, fully half the present state of New York—somewhat over 5 million acres—had been parceled out to only six individuals and land-jobbing companies for pennies per acre. When the operators engaging in such speculations turned their gaze to the national public domain (and it did not take long), circumstances conspired to enhance their opportunities. The Ordinance of 1785 itself, by stipulating that land auctions be held only in eastern cities, that no parcel smaller than 640 acres be offered for sale, and that the minimum purchase price was to be one dollar per acre, neatly eliminated the pioneering western farmer. Even if that worthy yeoman could have been present at the auctions, it was less than likely that he would ever want a parcel as large as 640 acres or be able to pay for it if he *did* want it. Land jobbers, however, were present, did want 640 acres (and more), and could afford the asking price. Moreover, the government of the United States, nearly strangled by seven years of war indebtedness and as yet not established in the world trading system, was desperate for income. Unsurprisingly, the public domain was regarded as a ready, if not major source of revenue. Writing in *The Federalist Papers* in 1788, James Madison outlined the theory: "It is now no longer a point of speculation and hope that the Western territory is a mine of vast wealth to the United States; and although it is not of such a nature as to extricate them from their present distresses, or for some time to come to yield any regular supplies for the public expenses, yet must it hereafter be able, under proper management, both to effect a gradual discharge of the domestic debt and to furnish, for a certain period, liberal tributes to the federal treasury."

Like his fellow Federalists Alexander Hamilton and John Jay, Madison was a cautious man. Others in the government were less reluctant to dip immediately into that "mine of vast wealth" to alleviate the public debt—particularly when some of them realized that their own situations might be improved in the process. Against this background occurred what nineteenth-century historian John Bach McMaster described as "the most shameful piece of land jobbery that ever disgraced our country," namely, the Ohio land speculation of the 1780s.

The scheme began innocently enough on March 1, 1786, when Brigadier General Rufus Putnam, chief engineer of the Revolutionary army, met with a group of war veterans in Boston's Bunch of Grapes Tavern and organized the Ohio Company of Associates, whose purpose was to utilize the nearly worthless government certificates of security they had been issued during the war as pay to

buy up to 1 million acres of Ohio Valley land and colonize it. The idea was simple: by accepting the certificates as payment, the United States government would be ridding itself of $1 million worth of paper debt in one fell swoop, and the veterans who formed the company (together with those thousands who were expected to subscribe to shares) would be able to use their certificates for something other than purposes of personal hygiene and at the same time be put in the way of something good when land values in the area rose, as surely they must.

Unfortunately, after nearly a year of advertisement and personal cajolery, the Associates had been able to raise only 250,000 of the necessary 1 million certificates. At that point, they reasoned that subscribers might be pried loose from their skepticism if Congress assured the company of the necessary expanse of land in advance. To that end they sent one of their members, the Reverend Manasseh Cutler, to New York early in 1787 to open negotiations with the Congressional Board of the Treasury, which until the creation of the General Land Office in 1812 was in charge of land-sale revenues. Cutler found a sympathetic listener in the Secretary of the Board, Colonel William Duer, who also was imaginative in helping the veterans. He suggested that perhaps Congress needed more incentive; if the Associates asked for not merely 1 million acres but, say, 6.5 million—1.5 million now and an option on an additional 5 million to be taken at some future date—perhaps then Congress would become so entranced with the notion of ultimately getting rid of more than $6 million worth of debt in a single transaction that it would go along. He and his two associates on the Board, Duer said, would do their utmost to persuade Congress in that direction; what was more, they would use their considerable influence to arrange liberal terms of credit and would further arrange for a loan so that the Associates could make the necessary down payment. In exchange, and of course there would be an exchange, the Associates would assign the 5 million acres of option land to Duer and a few of his colleagues, being "a number of the principal characters in the city" (as Cutler noted in his diary), who would form an organization called the Scioto Company. This latter transaction, Duer reminded Cutler, would and should be kept a "profound secret" from Congress—or at least from those members not in on the deal.

The entire proposal, of course, was a blatant violation of the spirit as well as the letter of the Ordinance of 1785: the land was not yet surveyed, no auctions would be held, and the payment in debt certificates, given the fact that their real value ranged between

Aspens touched by the light of a Wyoming sunset; part of the public land.

OVERLEAF: The remnants of one man's hope of land, near Santa Cruz, California.

eight and fifteen cents per dollar, would amount to considerably less than the one dollar an acre stipulated by the law. It also was irresistible, certainly to Cutler, who knew he needed Duer's support, and apparently to Congress, for at the end of July, 1787, the Ohio Purchase was approved. Payments were to be $500,000 in certificates upon the execution of the contract, another $500,000 when the entire tract of 6.5 million acres was surveyed into townships by the government, and the balance in six equal semiannual installments with interest. Title to the first 1.5 million acres would pass to the Associates upon receipt of the second payment of $500,000, and title to the option lands would pass upon such conditions as the Board of the Treasury and the Associates might negotiate.

Thus did nearly one-fourth of what would become the state of Ohio, some of the richest land on the American continent, pass from federal ownership. Not that it did the Ohio Company and its bastard child, the Scioto Company, much good; both had grossly overestimated the pace of settlement in the Ohio Valley. Not until 1794, when the Treaty of Greenville removed the Indians and Jay's Treaty with England removed British influence, did any significant rush to the interior begin. By 1792 the Ohio Company had induced only 230 families to settle on and buy its lands (and then only on credit); it could not make its second $500,000 payment and petitioned Congress for aid on the grounds that those who had settled the lands had done so in good faith and did not deserve to be evicted if title did not pass. Congress agreed, reducing the purchase price to such a level that the original down payment would satisfy the claim. Even with this helping hand, most of the company's directors, stretched thin in all directions, were forced to relinquish their shares in the enterprise to smaller and more secure speculators. The Scioto venture fared even worse; after several years of attempting to dodge (sell before purchasing) the option lands in France, with minimal success, the company simply dissipated, many of its members (including Duer) ending their lives in debtor's prison.

Both in their business practices, which were quite as shady as they were sharp, and in their ultimate failure, the Ohio and Scioto companies were typical of the large-scale raids on the public domain that proliferated from the Yazoo scandals of western Georgia to the Symmes Purchase of western Ohio in the ten years after 1785. For all their frenetic bluster, for all their inflated hopes, for all their sheer *size*, however, such exercises in kingdom-making were short-lived phenomena. As failure piled upon failure, the investment pool of eastern finance dried up. Moreover, Congress became much less roundheeled in its eagerness to accommodate such schemes when the revenue promised turned out to be considerably less than the "liberal tributes" that James Madison, among others, had anticipated. Speculation continued, but its form and substance changed, shaped now by a movement whose strength grew geometrically as settlement spilled across the Alleghanies into the bottomlands of the Ohio country, through the Cumberland Gap into Kentucky and Tennessee, and down the valley of the Mississippi.

One of the earliest and most persistent demands placed upon the public domain was that it could—and should—provide "land for the landless." This concept, while hardly unique to America, found its fullest and most significant expression in this country's western lands. Its imperatives influenced the nation's politics, its economics, and the very course of its history for seventy-five years, and the images it evoked spoke to something deeply important to the American character. Americans, that concept and its images said, were destined by God, Providence, or Fate—give it any name you wish—to be a nation of freeholders, upright, self-sufficient tillers of the soil, village-makers and country-builders. "Cultivators of the earth," Thomas Jefferson wrote in 1812, "are the most valuable citizens. They are the most vigorous, the most independent, the most virtuous, and they are tied to their country and wedded to its liberty and interests, by the most lasting bonds." Writing thirty years later, Henry Clay was hardly less enthusiastic. "Pioneers," he said, "penetrate into the uninhabited regions of the West. They apply the axe to the forest, which falls before them, or the plough to the prairie, deeply sinking its share in the unbroken wild grasses in which it abounds. They build houses, plant orchards, enclose fields, cultivate the earth, and rear up families around them."

There was much truth in the idea that the West—the public domain—was settled by men who found a definition of themselves in the land and whose sober strength was given to the nation —enough truth that the image has persisted to our own day. There also was a good deal that was false in it, for in many respects the world of the western settler was a feral, insecure one, a world dominated by speculation, greed, and credit—always credit. And if the settler justifiably protested that he was the victim of a government generally indifferent to his needs, of land jobbers willing to gouge him at every turn, and of bankers whose hearts were of polar ice, it may also be said that he was quite as often the victim of his own speculative instincts and the urge for what we would call today upward mobility. For every horny-handed son of toil who earnestly reflected Clay's dictum that he "build houses, plant orchards, enclose fields, cultivate the earth, and rear up families," there was at least one other who would have found more appeal in Charles C. Nott's proclamation fifty years later: "Go West, young man, go West, to make money to buy land to grow corn to fat hogs to make more money to buy more land to grow more corn to fat more hogs." Such men carried empires in their heads.

So it was that as Washington Irving's Ichabod Crane "rolled his great green eyes over the fat meadow-lands, the rich fields of wheat, of rye, of buckwheat, and Indian corn, and the orchard burdened with ruddy fruit, which surrounded the warm tenement of Van Tassel, his heart yearned after the damsel who was to inherit these domains, and his imagination expanded with the idea how they might be readily turned into cash and the money invested in immense tracts of wild land, and shingle palaces in the wilderness. Nay, his busy fancy realized his hopes, and presented to him the blooming Katrina, with the whole family of children, mounted on top of a wagon, loaded with household trumpery, with pots and kettles dangling beneath; and he beheld himself bestriding a pacing mare, with a colt at her heels, setting out for Kentucky, Tennessee, or the Lord knows where." So it was that George Donner, a successful Illinois farmer and a man who had indeed reared up a family around him, could sell his lands in 1846, sew $10,000 into the housecoat of his wife, Tamsen, and with her and his three children set off for a dream called California—only to find a grisly end in the driving snows of a Sierra Nevada winter.

The corn-growers and hog-fatteners of the West were gamblers just as surely as if they had been string-tied riverboat entrepreneurs, and it was the public domain that provided the stakes. And it was the public domain they wanted. Why should it be, they wanted to know, that the eastern land jobber, the banker, the lawyer, the merchant, the politician should be granted a nearly exclusive right to "make a rise" on America's lands? Why should the honest settler be forced to buy his piece of the future for dollars an acre from men who had purchased theirs for pennies an acre? Why was it that the government seemingly granted "every facility to the rich without consulting the poor," as one of the poor put it? If the government would move to eliminate these bloodsucking middlemen, if it would reduce the 640-acre minimum purchase to a size the settler could handle, if it would allow land auctions on the frontier rather than in the eastern cities, if it would extend *credit*, beGod, at interest rates that were not carved out of a man's skin—if the government would do all this, then a man might be able to get himself a nice 80-acre plot and work it a few years until its products or the pressures of settlement increased its value to the point that he could sell at a handsome profit and move on to take up a really sizable piece of land somewhere to the West. Out in western Illinois, maybe—they say it's going to be another Ohio one of these days. . . .

So went the original public domain, for as the settlers filled up the valleys of the trans-Appalachian West, as they carved out the states of Ohio, Indiana, Illinois, Kentucky, Tennessee, and Mississippi, as their economic and political influence swelled, their demands were listened to, and met. The first, if minor, reflection of this was the revision of the Ordinance of 1785 contained in the Land Act of 1796. Although this act, by raising the price per acre to two dollars and stipulating that half the public domain be sold off in tracts of no less than 5,760 acres, represented the views of speculators and eastern merchants who were afraid that their states would be depopulated if cheap land became available, there was a whisper of compromise with the West in the provision that created local land offices at Pittsburgh and Cincinnati.

On May 10, 1800, the whisper became something more—too much more in the eyes of some. The land act passed on that date, the result of the same forces that brought Thomas Jefferson to the presidency that year, was the first major expression of the West's increasing political clout. Under its provisions, the minimum number of acres that could be purchased was reduced to 320, and while the $2.00 purchase price remained in effect, remarkably liberal credit terms were offered: one-fourth of the purchase price due in forty days from the signing of contract, a second fourth in two years, a third in three years, and the remaining fourth in four years. In 1804 the act was further liberalized, the purchase price being reduced to $1.64 per acre and the minimum acreage reduced to 160.

The effect of the land acts of 1800 and 1804, predictably enough, was less to remove the public domain from the machinations of the speculator than to make it more possible for every man to be his own speculator. The result was inflation and land indebtedness to a spectacular degree, particularly in the years of the Great Migration west after the end of the War of 1812. Almost completely unregulated state banks were created by the hundreds to manufacture credit. Land values bloated to $50, $100, even $200

an acre, and the land jobber, far from the much-hated eastern ogre
of the earlier years, had become a pillar of the frontier community,
as Timothy Flint reported: "The speculators had a particular kind
of slang dialect . . . and when they walked about it was with an air
of solemn thoughtfulness upon their countenances as though wisdom would die with them. . . . A great and fortunate land
speculator and landholder was looked up to with as much venera-
tion by the people, as any partner in the house of Hope in London
or Gray in America." How could a man hate what he had every
expectation of becoming?

Inevitably, deflation followed inflation, an end that might have
been foreseen as early as 1806, when Congress passed the first of its
almost annual relief acts designed to postpone foreclosure on the
lands of greatly overextended settlers. In any case, by 1819 there
was no question about it. Banks collapsed like dominoes; panic
selling proliferated, and land values fell to below the original government purchase price; worthless deeds littered the gutters of
half-finished towns and anguished petitions pelted Congress from
those who blamed everything and everyone but themselves for
their plight. "All the flourishing cities of the West are mortgaged to
. . . the money power," Senator Thomas Hart Benton of Missouri
declared. "They may be devoured by it at any moment. They are in
the jaws of the Monster. A lump of butter in the mouth of a dog
—one gulp, one swallow, and all is gone!" An alarmed Secretary of
the Treasury reported that of the $47 million contracted for in the
sale of nearly 20 million acres of government land since 1796, more
than $17 million remained in uncollected and probably uncollect-
able debts. Congress reacted to all this by promptly foreclosing on
more than 5 million acres of mortgaged land and passing the Land
Act of 1820, which lowered the purchase price to $1.25 and re-
duced the minimum plot size to eighty acres, both of which were
provisions that the West could welcome, except that payment had
to be in cash—no credit.

The Act of 1820 was at least partially successful in that it
discouraged the kind of unbridled speculation that had brought the
West low, but its no-credit stipulation worked a miserable hardship
on the little man, at least in his own view. The $100 necessary for
the purchase of eighty acres would not have been an impossible
figure during normal times. But these were not normal times. Credit in the private sector, given the number of crippled and crum-
bled banks, was not only tight, but strangled. This left the land, and
those who lived on it, at the mercy of the "money monster" once
again, and the resentment that lived in such an interpretation grew

*The "Three Sisters," one of time's many sculptures
that punctuate the landscape of the American land.*

until it climaxed with the arrival of westerner Andrew Jackson to the White House in 1828.

Riding on his homespun coattails came an idea, a western idea. It was called pre-emption and it stemmed from the desires of those who, contrary to all existing law, had ventured out beyond the surveyed lands, beyond the immediate reach of even the speculator, and had settled what could only be called wilderness. We have learned to know them as pioneers. In their own time, they were also less elegantly described as squatters, and it is instructive to remember that in the late eighteenth and early nineteenth centuries even the term "pioneers" was a generally derogatory one, used to denote a seedy, unreliable, and probably unsanitary bunch of people who had turned their backs on civilization and chosen the life of savages. But the respectability of any group of people engaged in any activity tends to increase in direct proportion to their number (i.e., political influence), at least in American society, and by the time of Jackson's election in 1828 squatterism in the West had become more than an activity; it was an institution, and had to be treated as such.

Pre-emption was its child. Simply stated, what pre-emption would grant the squatter was the exclusive right to buy the land he had settled at a minimum price, thus removing the possibility of his being evicted from land that presumably he had cleared, broken, and carved into a home with his bare hands (as many did) by some Johnny-come-lately who happened to be at the right auction at the right time with the right amount of cash. The idea had been voiced in Congress periodically since the Land Law of 1796, but it did not receive serious attention until Jackson's administration, when the attention it received was serious indeed. In 1830 Congress passed its first Pre-emption Act, which entitled any settler who had cultivated a tract of land on the public domain by no later than the end of 1829 to claim any number of acres up to a maximum of 160 and buy it from the government for $1.25 an acre. The Act was to expire in two years, but that fact did not deter the western pioneer, who continued to hunker down on public-domain lands in 1830 and 1831, and petitioned Congress regularly: if the settler of 1829 deserved the right of pre-emption, why not the settler of 1830 and 1831? Under such pressure, Congress had little choice but to renew the Pre-emption Act in 1832, and again in 1834, 1838, and 1840. Finally, on August 30, 1841, the Pre-emption Act was made a permanent part of American land legislation.

The success of the pre-emption movement was a clear triumph of West over East in political terms, but it was no economic panacea for the frontier. It worked well enough; indeed, it might be said that it worked too well, for like the land laws of 1800 and 1804, its implementation encouraged speculation's myriad bubbles. Land easily obtained was land easily put to the great game of jobbery, and there was some justification for the assessment of Horace Greeley, editor of the *New York Tribune*, in 1843: "We said then [in 1841, opposing pre-emption legislation], what we repeat, that the preemption system, with its facility of trespassing on the public lands, is a curse to the West and to the whole country." Even while pre-emption had been considered a "temporary" expedient, it had contributed significantly to the nearly unrestrained land boom of the mid-1830s that spread throughout Michigan, Wisconsin Territory, Iowa Territory, Indiana, Illinois, Missouri, Arkansas, Mississippi, and Louisiana, complete with the standard frauds, squabbles, corruption of state and territorial legislatures and local branches of the General Land Office, and all the other paraphernalia of land fever. Congress, by then firmly in the grip of the disposal ethic, had not helped matters much; between 1834 and 1837 it had dumped more than 37 million acres of the public domain on the market, for sale either through pre-emption rights or through the provisions of the Land Law of 1820. This typical boom ended in 1837 with the typical depression—failed banks, individual bankruptcies, foreclosed mortgages—cooled a bit through the interruption of the Mexican War from 1846 to 1848, then was revived in the 1850s in full flower, enhanced by millions of acres in 160-acre military grants (to veterans of the war), most of which were sold to speculators, and by the Graduation Act of 1854, which allowed the sale of surveyed lands that had remained unsold for more than ten years at prices that ranged downward from $1.00 per acre for those unsold for ten years to only 12.5 cents per acre for those unsold for more than thirty years. Most of this land, too, fell into the hands of speculators.

So sublime in principle. . . . Between 1785 and 1860, the original public domain of the United States, that patrimony to be dispensed "for the common benefit," had disappeared down a path of good intentions littered with venality, speculation, and it must be said, irresponsibility. Three hundred million acres—gone. But there was more land, a whole continent of land left; and even as the agony of Civil War threatened to rip the nation apart, the pioneers and politicians, the land jobbers and entrepreneurs. fixed their fascinated gaze on the land west of the prairie, the land that stretched out until it was lost against the sky.

III
THE
GREAT
BARBECUE

FOR ALL ITS WEAKNESSES and probably inescapable subversions, the land system that evolved so painfully between the Ordinance of 1785 and the Pre-emption Act of 1841 had exhibited a recognizable logic in its attempt to rationalize the needs of the nation, of the emerging states, of the genuine settler, and the needs—or at least the caterwauling demands—of the speculator's instinct. (The needs of the land itself, of course, had been irrelevant. To very few was land a resource, and to almost no one was it an experience; it was still a commodity.) If various exercises in fraud and corruption and an almost chronic bad-debt condition systematically cheated the government of a fair price for the public domain, the revenue from land sales, particularly during the boom periods of the 1830s and 1850s, not only helped eliminate the national debt for one of the very few times in American history but also created a surplus, most of which was distributed to the states. If the generations of the future were denied their share in the 300 million acres that had slipped away, those acres at least had encouraged settlement and development and had gone toward the creation of a new American civilization in the wilderness. If the honest settler too often found himself at the mercy of banks and speculators, weighed down by debts that might take years to eradicate, his patrimony of 160 acres was at least a valid economic unit, from which he might reasonably expect to prosper as hard work on good land can make men prosper.

That logic, flawed even when it had been applied to the eastern third of the nation, simply disintegrated when measured against the nearly 1 billion acres of public domain that lay between the Mississippi River and the Pacific Slope. This trans-Mississippi

45

Dream as commodity: Like a footnote to history, a worn sign in the Mojave Desert of Southern California suggests a certain irony in the vision of "land for the landless."

West was a land outside the American experience, whose scope could only be imagined and whose complexity was not even suspected. To some, this was the Great American Desert, the Sahara of the North American continent, unfit for man and only barely fit for beast. After his exploring expedition of 1805 to 1809, Lieutenant Zebulon Montgomery Pike dismissed it from consideration: "In regard to this extensive section of country, I do not hesitate in giving the opinion that it is almost wholly unfit for cultivation, and of course uninhabitable by a people depending upon agriculture for their subsistence." To others, the land was a garden of all possible earthly delights; speaking before the Fenian Brotherhood in Denver, Colorado Territory, on July 4, 1868, territorial governor William Gilpin almost became unhinged at the prospect of this immense garden, this Fertile Crescent of America, this very heartland of the American future: "What an immense geography has been revealed! What infinite hives of population and laboratories of industry have been electrified and set in motion! . . . North America is known. . . . Its concave form and homogeneous structure are revealed."

Well, no. Neither the land's concavity, whatever Gilpin may have meant by the term, nor its homogeneity was known—the latter because it simply did not exist. The land was neither desert nor garden; it was both. It was short-grass plains and mountain meadows; full-flowing, contentious rivers and windblown arroyos; rain forests and sagebrush flats; alkaline sinks and timbered mountains; lush bottomlands and rock-ribbed, tumbling-down plateaus. In its size and variety, the land confounded logic. But the logic persisted in spite of evidence, experience, and common sense, and the western domain became the largest and juiciest morsel on the menu of what historian Vernon L. Parrington called The Great Barbecue of the nineteenth century.

In January, 1820, after the Missouri Compromise prohibited the extension of slavery in the territory of the United States north of Missouri's southern latitudinal boundary (36°30'), John Quincy Adams confided to his diary that "I take it for granted that the present question is a mere preamble—a title-page to a great, tragic volume." The great, tragic volume would not be complete until the meeting between Grant and Lee at Appomattox Court House more than forty-five years later, but in its earlier pages was written much of the history of the western movement for land reform. As the South began jockeying with the North in the game of power during the first years of the nineteenth century, it had found it convenient to ally itself with the growing West to shore up its political power. The price of the West's support for the South's "peculiar institution" and her desire for a low tariff had been the liberalization of the land laws, and the alliance had been a major factor in the movement that culminated with the Pre-emption Act of 1841.

By 1850, however, the situation had changed considerably. It was becoming increasingly apparent to the South that the dictates of geography and climate would prevent the extension of a plantation economy—whose foundation was slave labor—into the trans-Mississippi West. That West, it seemed, would become a land of small farmers. Moreover, its more natural ally would be the North, not the South, for a rapidly developing transportation network assured a steady flow of goods and services between the two; the North needed the timber, minerals, and agricultural products of the West, and the West needed the clothes and manufactures of the North, not to mention its investment money. As the capstone to this new alliance, the North, blessed with an ample labor supply through massive immigration from Germany and Ireland in the 1840s, no longer trembled at the prospect of the West's draining away its workingmen and began looking with favor upon the West's continuing demands for cheaper and more available cuts from the pie of the public domain.

Paranoid by instinct and self-persuasion, the South reacted to the West-North alliance by exercising every political tool at its disposal to block any further revision of the land laws and indulged in the rhetoric of fear. Writing in *Hunt's Merchants' Magazine* in 1851, one southern advocate noted the "tendency in the North to radicalism," pointing with alarm at the region's support of western demands for land reform, "a proposal to give away the public domain to the squatters of all nations and colors; 'the giving every man a farm' principle. Some of its advocates contend that the division shall not end with the public lands, but shall ultimately extend to the private; and antirentism is but one form of this claim." Another Southerner, writing in 1855, asserted: "Every year in the North a larger number is supported by the alms of the states. The criminal statistics show a frightful increase in crime, especially in the offenses against property; the right to gratuitous education by the forced taxes of the property holder is already a part of the public law, and societies are formed to establish a similar right to an equal division of lands. They declare that the earth is the gift of God for the common use—that no one has a right to monopolize it for himself and his posterity—and that every man

OVERLEAF: On the High Plains was an empire of grass waiting to be used—and by some, used up.

has a natural claim to an equal share in its enjoyment. The next step is to deny the right to transmit any kind of property by will or by inheritance, and to force a general redivision in every generation, if not an entire community of ownership."

Proclaiming the radicalism of such notions that "the earth is the gift of God for the common use," the South struggled to resist land reform, but at best its efforts were no more than stalling actions. In 1854 its opposition managed to kill the first attempt on the part of the West to pass a bill that incorporated the homestead principle—that the public land should be made as "free" as possible to the genuine settler—but could not stop passage of the Graduation Act of that same year. Under that law's provisions, all public lands that had been in the market for ten years or more and still were unsold were to be put up for sale: $1.00 an acre for those unsold for ten to fourteen years; 75 cents for those unsold for fifteen to nineteen years; 25 cents for twenty to twenty-nine years; and 12.5 cents for thirty years or more. In its opposition, the South predicted that the lands so distributed would fall into the hands of speculators rather than the common man, in line with tradition. The prediction was correct. During the land boom that swept west and north through Wisconsin, Iowa, and Minnesota after passage of the Graduation Act, 30 to 40 million acres a year were sold to speculators, more than one-third of the acreage at the 12.5-cent price.

Correct or not, the South was in a losing fight. Early in 1859 the House of Representatives passed a homestead bill by a vote of 120 to 76. Frantic action in the Senate on the part of its southern members managed to get the bill tabled for the remainder of the session, but by a vote of only 29 to 28. In February, 1860, an identical bill was once again introduced in the House, passing this time by 115 to 65. Southern manipulations in the Senate kept the bill from coming to a vote for more than two months, but on May 11 it was passed, 44 to 8. A little more than one month later, President James Buchanan vetoed the bill on the grounds that it was unconstitutional because nothing in that document specifically authorized the federal government to give lands away (thus ignoring the provisions of the Ordinances of 1785 and 1787, which with appropriate Congressional revision allowed the government to do pretty much as it wished with the public domain).

Buchanan's veto was the South's last stand against land reform. With the election of Abraham Lincoln in 1860, the consequent secession of the South, and the even more consequent shelling of Fort Sumter on April 12, 1861, the last major voice against the homestead principle was removed from Congress. On May 6, 1862, Congress passed the Homestead Act, and on May 20 President Lincoln signed it, giving form to his own earlier statement that "I am in favor of settling the wild lands into small parcels so that every poor man may have a home." In the terms of the act, any head of household or person over twenty-one years of age (including aliens who had declared their intention of becoming citizens) had a right to 160 acres of the surveyed public domain. Full title could be attained by residing on the land for a period of five years, by improving it (building a house on the land or cultivating it), and by the payment of a fee of $34.00 on the Pacific Coast and $26.00 elsewhere. Earlier title could be acquired after visible improvement and a residence of six months—and a payment at the pre-emption price of $1.25 an acre. An affidavit required of the settler stipulated that his application for land was "for his or her exclusive use and benefit" and that it was "for the purpose of actual settlement and cultivation, and not, either directly or indirectly,. for the use or benefit of any other person or persons whomsoever." Horace Greeley, long an advocate of land reform, applauded his country "on the consummation of one of the most beneficent and vital reforms ever attempted in any age or clime—a reform calculated to diminish sensibly the number of paupers and idlers and increase the proportion of working, independent, self-subsisting farmers in the land evermore."

So there it was—the concept of land for the landless given the definition of law. Of law, but not of reality: the Homestead Act of 1862, quite as revolutionary in intent as the South had feared and as Horace Greeley had celebrated, may well have been one of those ideas whose time had come—but too late. Its logic had been shaped by two-and-one-half centuries of experience in the well-watered, richly productive geography of the eastern third of the nation, and if it had come twenty or thirty or forty years earlier, it might have served its purpose well. But by 1862 the wedding of land with logic could no longer be made, in heaven or not. For the land that stretched west to the Continental Divide and beyond, for all its variety, did possess one unifying factor—aridity. Its most arable soils experienced less than twenty inches of rainfall a year. With irrigation, those soils could "blossom as the rose"; without it, they bloomed reluctantly, if at all. And in a land whose rivers were few and far between and whose waters often flowed "too thick to drink and too thin to plow," irrigation was no proposition for those poor men to whom Lincoln would have given homes; it was an expensive, time-consuming, and back-breaking business for which he

Homesteading: Many a sodbuster's wife was forced to
choke back her squeamishness in collecting and using the
land's basic fuel: buffalo chips. Most did, and for them
it was "out of the bread, into the chips, and back again
—and not even a dust of the hands!"

Decked out in their Sunday best, with all that they
had within sight of the camera's lens, these
sodhouse families of western Kansas (above and below)
placed their lives on the record for itinerant photographer A. A. Forbes in about **1890**.

had neither the money nor the experience. In short, those who chose to gamble their futures by homesteading a land that did not welcome them found their physical endurance and their minds and hearts tested to almost incredible limits, as Wallace Stegner has outlined in *Beyond the Hundredth Meridian*:

> Suppose a pioneer tried. Suppose he did (most couldn't) get together enough money to bring his family out to Dakota or Nebraska or Kansas or Colorado. Suppose he did (most couldn't) get a loan big enough to let him build the dwelling demanded by law, buy a team and a sodbuster plow and possibly a disc harrow and a seeder and perhaps a binder—whatever elements of the multiplying array of farm machinery he had to have. Suppose he managed to buy seed, and lay in supplies or establish credit for supplies during the first unproductive year. Suppose he and his family endured the sun and glare on the treeless prairie, and were not demolished by the cyclones that swept across the plains like great scythes. Suppose they found fuel in a fuelless country, possibly digging for it [as the fantasy-ridden William Gilpin had once suggested, claiming that the root system of the plains was a veritable year-round, inexhaustible woodlot], but more likely burning cow-chips, and lasted into fall, and banked their shack to the window sills with dirt against the winter's cold, and sat out the blizzards and the loneliness of their tundra-like home. Suppose they resisted cabin fever, and their family affection withstood the hard fare and the isolation, and suppose they emerged into spring again. It would be like emerging from a cave. Spring would enchant them with crocus and primrose and prairies green as meadows. It might also break their hearts and spirits if it browned into summer drouth. The possibilities of trouble, which increased in geometrical ratio beyond the hundredth meridian, had a tendency to materialize in clusters. The brassy sky of drouth might open to let across the fields winds like the breath of a blowtorch, or clouds of grasshoppers, or crawling armies of chinch bugs. Pests always seemed to thrive best in drouth years. And if drouth and insect plagues did not apear there was always a chance of cyclones, cloudbursts, hail.
>
> It took a man to break and hold a homestead of 160 acres even in the subhumid zone. It took a superman to do it on the arid plains. It could hardly, in fact, be done, though some heroes tried it.

Thousands of heroes—or potential heroes—did try it, beginning on January 2, 1863, with one Daniel Freeman of Beatrice, Gage County, Nebraska, whose entry was number one, whose proof of residence was number one, and whose patent (full title) was number one written on page one of book one of the United States General Land Office, Homestead Division. (Remarkably, Freeman was one of those who held out against the odds; as late as 1934, his homestead farm was still owned by his descendants). Native Americans and immigrants alike crowded into newly opened land offices as federal surveys crept west across the plains. In *The*

Northern Tier, E. Jeff Jenkins described one such land-office opening in Concordia, Kansas on January 16, 1871, a scene duplicated
in all its details hundreds of times in the twenty years and more
after passage of the Homestead Act: "The door was opened—a
shout—a rush—a scramble over each other—a confused shouting
of the number of the range and township, as a half-dozen or more
simultaneously presented their papers to the officers, who, in the
tumult, could as well have told which animal was the first taken
into the ark, as to have designated which one of the settlers was
prior in time with the presentation of his papers. . . . I shall never
forget that scene. The space outside the railing or counter was
instantly filled with settlers, until there was scarcely standing
room, and yet a very large number of the applicants failed to gain
admittance. Throughout the entire day, during office hours, the
number of applicants increased, and, at the close of business for the
day, a large number had failed to gain admittance. The day's work
footed up one hundred and six homesteads entered. . . . The officers and their clerks were obliged to work until a late hour at night
to transcribe the business transacted through the day. The following day was a repetition of the previous one, and the rush continued for months."

However enthusiastic such settlers may have been, most simply could not "prove up" against the hardships of climate and
geography. Of the 552,112 homestead entries filed between 1862
and 1882 (comprising more than 54 million acres), only 194,488
were held to full title, either through five-year residences or six-
month commutation at $1.25 an acre, as the following table illus-
trates:

Homestead Entries, 1862–1882

	ORIGINAL ENTRIES		FINAL ENTRIES	
	Entries	*Acres*	*Entries*	*Acres*
Alabama	28,995	2,875,547.12	5,227	542,147.69
Arkansas	44,940	4,095,743.94	11,562	1,142,623.01
California	24,750	3,218,745.16	10,012	1,235,213.09
Dakota	52,733	8,142,999.85	7,806	1,142,263.71
Florida	16,390	1,743,331.41	3,305	353,702.91
Kansas	86,936	11,746,949.80	34,055	4,660,734.83
Minnesota	70,616	8,473,058.89	31,610	3,672,710.61
Mississippi	12,489	1,175,037.45	2,094	203,410.86
Nebraska	64,328	8,183,076.25	29,140	3,566,477.29
Oregon	11,710	1,544,526.43	4,017	551,284.02
Washington	12,668	1,675,162.92	3,360	436,246.96

Pawing and bellowing like the very hounds of hell, Texas longhorns are prodded into cattle cars in Sedalia, Kansas in 1871. Somewhat more docile, the creatures in the Montana herd below are doing what cattle do best: eating grass.

This is not to say that the Homestead Law did not use up its share of the western public domain. It did—to the extent of more than 80 million acres by 1900. Yet less than one-third of this amount remained in the hands of the honest settler. The rest, it should come as no surprise, went to those to whom it had always gone in the manner in which it had nearly always gone: to those who needed it least, by means more often foul than fair.

If the pioneering farmer generally could not take advantage of the land offered him by the Homestead Act, there were those who could. Chief among them was the rancher, the integer of what became known, somewhat grandly, as the Cattle Kingdom. At the end of the Civil War, Texas cattlemen contemplated the nearly 6 million head of longhorn cattle in the state, further contemplated the fact that even the stringiest piece of meat on the hoof sold for $35 a head in the railhead town of Sedalia, Missouri, even further contemplated the sorry condition of their fortunes after nearly five years of war, and came to a simple conclusion: take the meat to market. Beginning in 1865 thousands of cattle a year were herded north in spring drives over the skein of drovers' paths that came to be known collectively as the Chisolm Trail, first to Sedalia, later to Abilene and Dodge City, Kansas. It was no small affair; between 1868 and 1871, 1.5 million head of cattle were received for rail shipment at Abilene alone.

As railroad development pushed across the Mississippi and Missouri rivers and nosed west to the very edge of the western domain, the cattle industry moved to the next reasonable step: instead of burning the meat off the animals by herding them up from Texas over trails choked with dust, why not simply raise them closer to market? Within a handful of years, consequently, much of the Great Plains, from about the southern border of Kansas to the northern border of Montana, from the Missouri River to the Rocky Mountains, had been converted into an immense pasture, which by 1880 held more than 6 million cattle. Too many cattle, in fact: the total number of acres of the seven states through which the Great Plains ran (Kansas, Nebraska, South Dakota, North Dakota, Montana, Wyoming, and Colorado) amounted to about 422 million acres, or a little over 72 acres for every head of cattle. Given the fact that much of this territory was comprised of mountains and other land unfit for grazing and much of it was under cultivation, the number of acres per animal was certainly much lower, almost surely lower than the 30 to 40 acres normally capable of supporting a single cow. The result was overgrazing, during which the grasslands were stripped quite as efficiently as if the cattlemen had set a match to them in a high summer wind.

The country, of course, was at least two generations removed from anything that could be called a "land ethic," and the cattlemen were blind to anything but their faith that the land was something to be used, and if necessary, used up. The land in question was the public domain. During the earliest years of the range industry on the plains, land was controlled by nothing more complicated than the appropriation of a stream, spring, or other body of water (in a nearly waterless land, whoever controlled a working creek controlled precisely as much land around it as his cattle were willing to travel over to reach water), by gentlemen's agreements among ranching neighbors, and when and if those agreements were violated, by force. The government was not consulted. This wonderfully casual approach to the problem of land use worked well enough so long as the settlement line of the frontier remained east of the hundredth meridian. When it crossed that line, problems began to develop—such inconvenient matters as the question of legal title to the land, the right of others for a share in it, that sort of thing.

Until it became politically inexpedient, the range industry was inclined to handle the problem of the homesteader—or "nester," as cattlemen were wont to call him—by means of direct confrontation, and the resulting violence in such conflicts as the Johnson County "war" of Wyoming in 1883 became part of the American folklore. Yet for all the bloodshed—real and apochryphal—that accompanied the clash between the rangeland culture and the sodbusting culture on the Great Plains, probably the greatest violence was done the Homestead Law. The cattleman was a raw pragmatist, and it did not take him long to realize that he could twist the provisions of the law to his own ends. The government insisted that he possess legal title to the grasslands he had come to believe were his by more-or-less divine right? So be it. Gangs of hired hands —otherwise known as cowboys—were assigned the duty (often as a condition of employment) of filing homestead claims, "residing" on their 160-acre parcels for six months, then buying them (with their employers' money) at the commutation price of $1.25 an acre and assigning title immediately to their benefactors. Residence was proved by swearing to the existence of a "twelve by fourteen dwelling," neglecting to mention the fact that the measurement was in inches, not feet, by renting a portable cabin for five dollars and hauling it to the claim in front of witnesses, or by tacking a pair of shingles to a canvas tent and swearing that the habitation was a

For all the romance that has crusted about his memory, the American cowboy was in fact only a little above the cow itself in the social scale of his time. Photographer A. A. Forbes caught these "hired hands on horseback" in 1890.

"shingled dwelling." Local land offices, understaffed and responsible for thousands of square miles of public domain, were neither equipped nor inclined to investigate the validity of individual claims. In this way, millions of acres of public lands went to fill out the holdings of Western ranch operations, many of which were immense corporate businesses owned by Eastern and European interests—all of this under the umbrella of a law that had been calculated, in Horace Greeley's words, to "increase the proportion of working, independent, self-subsisting farmers in the land evermore." (The cattleman got his comeuppance, in a manner of speaking, in the "Big Die" during the brutal winter of 1885 to 1886, the summer drouth that followed it, and a second heavy winter in 1887 to 1888; millions of cattle perished. This, combined with the widespread overgrazing that had depleted the grasslands in the 1870s and early 1880s, crippled the industry for the next generation; see Chapter 8.)

The cattleman was not alone in his blithe perversions of the law. Utilizing both the pre-emption and homestead laws as the cattleman used them, the homesteader's opposite number, the agri-industrialist, pieced together immense properties from the public domain to make "bonanza farms" whose fields of wheat glittered for mile after golden mile. These were not family farms; they were factories. Their land was broken by platoons of huge Stockton gang plows and harvested by squadrons of horse-drawn reapers and steam-driven threshers, and an army of laborers serviced them under the command of such men as Oliver Dalrymple, whose 13,000-acre wheat ranch in the Dakota Territory of the 1880s had pioneered the practice of large-scale production on the plains. The farmers who worked such operations were in no way related to Jefferson's independent yeomen; they were laborers just as surely as if they had been sweating out their lives in a Pittsburgh steel mill, and for them the land held neither joy nor prosperity.

The timber cutter found the homestead law equally bendable to his pursuits, and in describing his activities, depredation is not too strong a word. Many "tramp" lumbermen merely marched men and equipment onto a suitable isolated tract of timberland in the public domain, stripped it, and moved out, knowing full well that apprehension and prosecution were generally beyond the means of the overcommitted General Land Office. Others, more sensitive to the nobility of law, took advantage of the homestead and pre-emption statutes, for there was nothing in either of these that specifically excluded timberlands from "settlement." Filing a claim for himself and instructing his employees to go and do likewise, the

From cultivation to corporation: Above, a farmer reaps the harvest from his 160 acres of Minnesota land; below, steam-driven threshers and teams of laborers strip the wealth from a county-sized industrial wheat farm in western Kansas.

industrious lumber entrepreneur or mill man hauled his donkey engines and portable sawmill into an area that might comprise several thousand acres, cut everything that could be cut, then abandoned the claims without bothering to establish final title. Such instances of cheerful plunder had gutted many of the forests of the public domain as early as 1866, when the surveyors-general of both Washington Territory and Colorado Territory earnestly recommended to the General Land Office that the forest lands in their territories be sold immediately while there was anything left to sell. The lands were not sold, and millions, perhaps billions, of board feet of lumber disappeared in great swathes from public lands scattered from northern California to Florida (the only public-land state on the Eastern seaboard), again under the aegis of a supremely well-intentioned law designed to give every poor man a home in the wilderness.

The good intentions continued—but so did the subversions and depredations. In an attempt to rationalize the nation's demonstrably irrational land system, Congress passed three additions to the Homestead Act in the 1870s. The first of these, the Timber Culture Act of 1873, was a singularly fruitless effort to stimulate the growth of forests where forests could not be grown, and suggested a profound ignorance on the part of those who held the public domain in trust. This act allowed any homesteader to claim an adjoining 160 acres, to become his if he planted one-fourth of it in trees (later reduced to 10 acres) within four years. Like the Homestead Act itself, the Timber Culture Act would only have been workable in a humid or subhumid climate; the notion of attempting to nurse some spindly tree to maturity in the teeth of a high plains gale and in a climate that alternately burned it and froze it was absurd. That did not deter the speculators, ranchers, and bonanza wheat farmers, of course, who used the law to wonderful advantage. "My information," the Land Commissioner wrote in his 1885 report, "leads me to the conclusion that a majority of entries under the Timber Culture Act are made for speculative purposes, and not for the cultivation of the timber. Compliance with the law in these cases is a mere pretense and does not result in the production of timber. . . ." Furthermore, he went on, "Within the great stock ranges of Nebraska, Kansas, Colorado and elsewhere, one-quarter of nearly every section is covered by a timber-culture entry made for the use of the cattle owners, usually by their herdsmen who make false land-office affidavits as a part of the conditions of their employment." Ten million acres gone.

The second amendment to the Homestead Act was the Desert

Harvest of the mountains: This "cold deck" (winter supply) of California redwood logs represents more than five million board feet of lumber. Land is still money.

Land Act of 1877, almost certainly the child of the cattleman's lobby. This provided for the tentative title to 640 acres limited to the Great Plains and the Southwest (including California) by the payment of 25 cents an acre. If he could prove that he had irrigated the land within three years after filing, a man could then secure final title by paying an additional dollar an acre, and in the meantime he could transfer the tentative title (true also of the Timber Culture Act, though not of the Homestead Act). Needless to say, teams of cowboys were rounded up to file claims, buckets of water were dumped on the ground so that witnesses could honestly swear that they had "seen water on the claim," and titles were passed over to the ranch owners. Another 2,674,695 acres gone.[2]

The West's lumbermen got their own handy law with the third amendment to the Homestead Act, the Timber and Stone Act of 1878. This act applied only to those lands in California, Nevada, Oregon, and Washington that were "unfit for cultivation" and "valuable chiefly for timber and stone," and allowed any citizen or first-paper alien to claim and buy 160 acres of timberland for $2.50 an acre (not much less than the price of a single mill log then, and somewhat less than the $10,000 an acre that redwood land in California, for example, brings today). Historian Ray Allen Billington described what followed: "Company agents rounded up gangs of alien seamen in waterfront boarding houses, marched them to the courthouse to file their first papers, then to the land office to claim their quarter section, then to a notary public to sign over their deeds to the corporation, and back to the boarding houses to be paid off. Fifty dollars was the usual fee, although the amount soon fell to $5 or $10 and eventually to the price of a glass of beer." Another 3.6 million acres gone.

So went nearly one-tenth of the Western public domain under the provisions of the Homestead Act and its amendments—the ward of good intentions, the victim of greed, and hostage, finally, to a glass of beer.

While the General Land Office wrestled with the angel of the land laws entrusted to its supervision, and speculators, cattlemen, lumbermen, and bonanza farmers happily twisted those laws to fit their own purposes, Congress did not neglect other means of disposing of the public domain. One such was the Swamp Lands Act of 1850, another measure as sordid in application as it was reasonable in purpose. The act was inspired by the need for reclamation projects in such areas as the lands in the southern Mississippi Valley, where the great river had a habit of running amok on a yearly and fre-

A group of hopeful prospectors, full of fun and yeasty visions of the future, congregate in "Ocean Grove" near the San Miguel River of Colorado, 1885.

Ladies without Bloomers not allowed on the Beach
Tourists without Baggage in advance
O. G. DINING ROOMS - 16 TO: ONE
Ocean Grove

quently twice-yearly basis, and it granted all "swamp and over-flow" lands to the states in which they lay with the stipulation that "the proceeds of said lands shall be applied, exclusively, so far as necessary, to the purpose of reclaiming said lands by means of levees and drains." The act also provided that only such land as was specified on government maps to be "swamp and unfit for cultivation" could be granted, but the proviso was later eliminated, an action that effectively crippled any possibility that the act would be applied legitimately. Local speculators and land monopolists, of course, had little difficulty in persuading state legislators to classify valuable agricultural and grazing land as swamps unfit for cultivation, selling it to them at $1.25 an acre, then refunding the money upon their sincere claim that they had spent a like amount on reclamation. In California alone, one man—"Cattle King" Henry Miller—so competently manipulated the law with the connivance of accommodating state legislators that he acquired a hundred-mile strip of land on both sides of the San Joaquin River in the state's Central Valley, and over the nation more than 80 million acres were appropriated through similar flights of chicane.

Similarly noble in intent, the Morrill Land-Grant Act of 1862 was an extension of the sentiment that had set aside one section of each surveyed township for the support of public schools in the Ordinance of 1785. First introduced by Representative Justin S. Morrill of Vermont in 1857, the act was passed the following year by both houses, but was vetoed by President James Buchanan, reflecting, as he usually did, the desires of the South. It was revived after the beginning of the Civil War, passed again, and signed into law by Lincoln on July 2, 1862. It granted to each state (except those in the Confederacy) 30,000 acres for each senator and representative in Congress, the proceeds from the sale of such lands to go toward the endowment of at least one college in each state whose purpose, "without excluding other scientific and classical studies, and including military tactics," would be to "teach such branches of learning as are related to agriculture and mechanic arts . . . in order to promote the liberal and practical education of the industrial classes in the several pursuits and professions in life." Those states that possessed no public lands would be issued scrip to the tune of $1.25 an acre for their allotments, which could be located anywhere in the West where there was no competing claim. Unlike the Swamp Land Act, the Morrill Land-Grant Act did bring concrete results, as the scores of agricultural colleges scattered over the country attest; yet, like the lands granted by the reclamation act, those granted under the terms of the Morrill

Land-Grant Act quickly disappeared into the hands of various entrepreneurs, often at prices considerably and conveniently lower than the $1.25 required by law. More than 130 million acres disappeared, in fact.

The General Mining Law of 1872 was less a matter of dispensing with undisposed public lands than a belated recognition of lands already appropriated. With the exception of iron and lead deposits in Minnesota and coal deposits in Iowa, the public lands for more than sixty years after 1785 had revealed few mineral resources, and as a consequence neither Congress nor the General Land Office had contrived a workable means of regulating mining activity on the public domain. Deprived of any federal guidelines, miners simply developed their own, beginning with those in the California Gold Rush of 1848 to 1852, which saw more than forty thousand men scuttling like so many beetles on a corpse over the western slopes of the Sierra Nevada. In placer (surface) mining the system was simple enough. The claim was comprised of a square or rectangle of ground of locally specified dimensions, into which the miner could dig clear to bedrock and beyond if he chose. To regulate the filing and development of such claims, miners in any given region formed themselves into districts and pieced together a code of laws regarding claim sizes, requirements of registration, and the minimum development work a man had to maintain on his claim to hold title to it (such as laboring on it "one day out of every three"). Lode (subsurface) mining was a more complicated matter, but again California miners came up with a solution, maintaining that ownership of the surface part of a lode vein, or apex, gave the miner the right to follow that vein, together with all its "dips, spurs, angles, and variations" as deep and as far as it led him. With local variations the system devised in California was carried into all the pockets and crannies of the mining West in the 1850s and 1860s, and it was given a congressional imprimatur in 1866 by a law that declared the mineral lands of the public domain, surveyed or not, to be "free and open to exploration and occupation by all citizens of the United States, and those declaring their intention to become citizens, subject to . . . the local customs or rules of miners in the several mining districts, so far as the same are not in conflict with the laws of the United States."

This was a little loose even in the great age of a *laissez-faire* economy, and the Mining Law of 1872 was somewhat more stringent, setting up a schedule for the sale, rather than donation, of mineral lands—$2.50 an acre for placer claims and $5.00 an acre for lode claims—again "subject to . . . the local customs or rules of miners in the several mining districts. . . ." With few revisions, this

OVERLEAF: Black Hawk, Colorado, in about 1800 part of the future dreamed of by the prospectors on page 65.

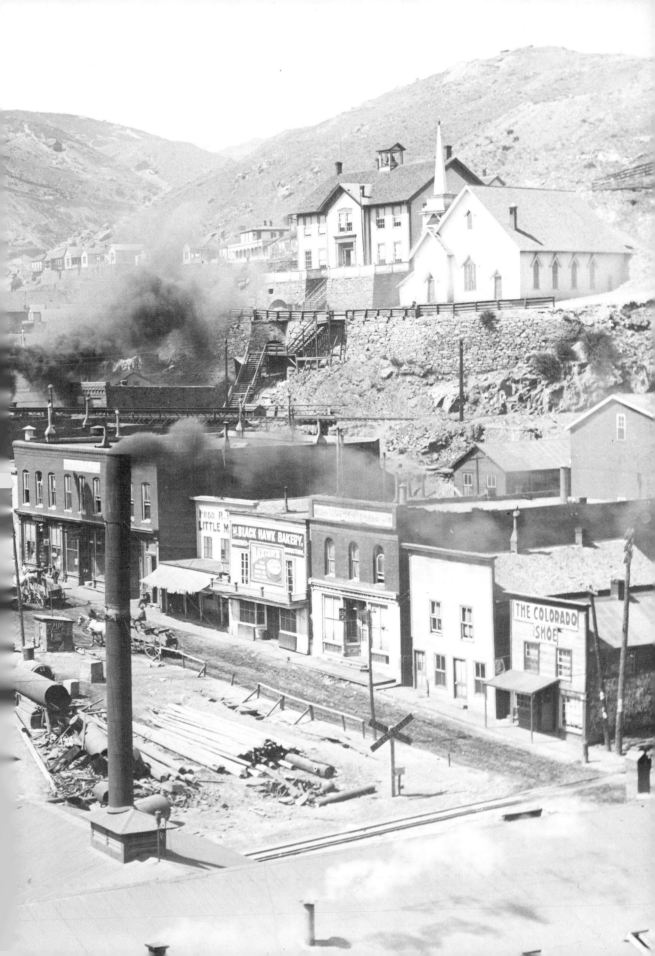

remains the basic law of mining on the public domain. How much of the national inheritance vanished before and after the Mining Law of 1872? No one has been enough of a masochist to calculate the acreage with any certainty, but it may be instructive to note that during the years 1860 to 1880 in the Comstock District of Nevada alone, no fewer than 17,000 individual claims were filed, many of them legitimate, in spite of Mark Twain's dictum that "a western mine is a hole in the ground owned by a liar."

And then there were the Indian lands, the patrimony of those people of the stone age who met the people of the iron age head-on—and lost. There would have been no public domain, of course, if the federal government had not systematically arranged for the dispossession of the Indians from the Western lands. It did so at the insistence of people who wanted those lands, and did so with little competence but with a kind of leaden inexorability. It did so by treaty—more than 370 treaties between 1774 and 1871—when it could, and by force when nothing else would work. It did so humanely at times, and more often with a brutal directness, but never without a sense of guilt that is with us yet. (For more on this and other aspects of the relationship between the Indian and the public domain, see Chapter 11.) By 1850 most of the Indians, by one means or another, had been removed from the Mississippi and Ohio river valleys, many assigned to the Indian Territory that had been established in the area that would become the state of Oklahoma. And by 1870 most of the Indians west of the Mississippi and Missouri rivers had been confined to reservations scattered from Washington Territory to Kansas under the not always enlightened care of the Bureau of Indian Affairs and its agents. These reservations comprised a total of about 138 million acres and were presumably to be held in trust for them "for as long as the grass shall grow and the rivers shall run," in the traditional language of agreements with Indians. Equally traditional was the impermanence of such promises, for it was not long before the pressures of the continuing westward movement began nibbling away at the Indian reserves. "The Indian lands are the best in the state," the Bureau of Indian Affairs (BIA) agent for the Osage River Reservation of Kansas wrote in 1864, "and justice would demand, as well as every consideration of policy and humanity, that these fertile lands should be thrown open to settlement, and the abode of civilized and industrious men." The governor of Colorado Territory, Edward M. McCook, echoed that sentiment in 1870, proclaiming that "God gave to us the earth, and the fulness thereof, in order that we might utilize and enjoy His gifts. I do not believe in donating to these indolent savages the best portion of my territory, and I do not believe in placing the Indians on an equality with the white man as landholders."

How could indolent savages argue with such compelling logic? They could not, of course, except through vain and short-lived skirmishes, and one by one Indian reservations were reduced or eliminated entirely, their occupants paid off by the government (payments were normally handled by BIA officials by the allotment of food and clothing, not money), moved either to the Indian Territory or to other reservations, and the freed land opened to settlement. In 1887, the Dawes Severalty Act accelerated the dismemberment of Indian reservations by allowing individual Indians to claim tentative title to plots of reservation land (160 acres for a head of household, 80 acres for a single male over the age of twenty-one) in a benighted attempt to make Apollonian farmers of Dionysian hunters; reservation land not so claimed was declared open for settlement. The climax to all this came in 1889, when most of the Indian Territory itself was purchased from the Indians, renamed Oklahoma Territory, and exposed to the mercies of land "boomers" from all over the West—"all the elements of western life," as one observer noted, "a wonderful mixture of thrift and unthrift, of innocence and guile, of lambs and wolves." Between the end of the Civil War and 1890, nearly 100 million acres of the public domain that had been assigned to the American Indian "in perpetuity" had been lost not only to the Indian but to all Americans.

It was indeed "The Great Barbecue," this forty-year raid on the public domain. Pre-emption lands, homestead lands, desert-act lands, timber-culture lands, swamplands, college-grant lands, mineral lands, timber and stone lands, Indian lands, lands sold outright . . . more than 400 million acres had been served up and consumed in one of the most profligate and shortsighted examples of territorial gluttony recorded in the annals of history. Nor was the meal complete; another course—dessert, perhaps?—remains to be accounted for.

IV
EVERY MOUNTAIN SHALL BE MADE LOW

THERE WAS SOMETHING IN THE AMERICA of the nineteenth century that responded to the image of a steam locomotive and its train thundering across the landscape. It was the Great Machine of the era; the lyric melancholy of its whistle spoke of progress and enterprise, of muscle, money, and the technological coming of age of America, and more; it spoke also of adventure, of the romance of the far-off, of dreams made possible and real. That sound, wailing in the darkness of a high-plains midnight, or lost in the empty sage of South Pass, or echoing from the canyons of the Wasatch, was the theme song for a nation of wanderers.

That age is now gone, of course, and even its romance has been dimmed by the ages that followed it—the Automobile Age, the Air Age, the Jet Age, and now, unless we are careful, the threshold of the Supersonic Age. Yet even in recollection a hint of the original magic remains, for the railroad was a deeply personal extension of its time; its meaning and purpose were clear; its engines of progress were *understandable* machines. There is a residue of that sense of identification left in us today, for the railroad was one of the prime symbols of a time we like to recall as being simpler and less demanding than our own, one more evocative of what we still call the American Dream. So it is that the manufacturers of singularly unromantic diesel locomotives spend a remarkable amount of money and time attempting to duplicate the sound of the old steam engine's whistle (imperfectly); so it is that country-western singer Johnny Cash can present an hour-long railroad special on national

73

Windmill and engine at Laramie, Wyoming, in 1868—one of the main stops on the Union Pacific's road to Promontory.

television to his and the network's profit, recreating in songs and living dioramas some of the more splendid moments in the history of the national memory.

It is necessary to recognize the force of that image—in its own way every bit as powerful as the image of the yeoman farmer —before we can begin to understand how it was that in the 1860s the Congress of the United States could be persuaded to part with more than $100 million in federal loans (most of which was not repaid for more than forty years, and then under duress) and more than 90 million acres of the public domain, a national gift taken from the national lands by the national government and given outright to a handful of empire-builders—men with the foresight, shrewdness, unenlightened self-interest, and raw determination to turn great dreams to their own ends.

The process began as early as the 1820s, and like almost every other manifestation of national land use, it began with an idea of demonstrable virtue. The idea was called "internal improvements," and what it involved was the financing of canals, wagon roads, and river and harbor improvements through the sale of public lands. Unlike many other concepts of national land use, this one received almost no opposition. The necessity of such improvement to regional and national growth and the inability of most states and territories to pay for them without help were obvious. Speaking at Faneuil Hall in 1828, Daniel Webster—acknowledged spokesman for New England, a region never noted for its enthusiasm for giving *anything* away—articulated a nearly uncontested argument: "Some of these undertakings have been attended with great expense, and have subjected the States . . . to large debts and heavy taxation. The lands of the United States, being exempted from all taxation, of course, bear no part of this burden. Looking at the United States, therefore, as a great landed proprietor, essentially benefited by these improvements. I have felt no difficulty in voting for appropriation of parts of these lands, as a reasonable contribution by the United States to these general objects."

While obviously not one of his more impressive flights of eloquence, Webster's Boston speech captured a national inclination in mid-passage, and over the next two decades public lands in relatively small quantities were granted to various states, and from them to various private canal and wagon-road companies, for the construction of various "general objects." Inevitably, as the lines of the nation's embryonic railroad system began edging westward, the land-grant concept was not long in being applied to an industry that was revolutionizing overland transportation. (In 1830 there were only 23 miles of railroads in the United States; by 1840 there were more than 2,800, and by 1850 more than 9,000.) Railroads and internal improvements rapidly became synonymous terms. Reflecting this, on September 20, 1850, Congress passed a Railroad Act, which granted to the states of Illinois, Alabama, and Mississippi alternate sections of the public domain six miles in width (adding up to 3,840 acres per mile) along either side of railroad rights-of-way to be determined by the states involved. In 1851 Illinois transferred its land grant, which ultimately totaled 2,572,800 acres, to the Illinois Central Railroad, and in the same year Alabama and Mississippi assigned their total of 1,156,569 acres to the Mobile and Ohio Railroad. In 1852 Congress went a step further, passing a general right-of-way act that granted to any railroad corporation for the following ten years a 100-foot right-of-way through public lands—including the right to use timber for construction and sale—providing that any railroad receiving such a grant complete its line within fifteen years from the date of the allocation.

The combination of the Railroad Act of 1850 and the Right-of-Way Act of 1852 affected the ever-present pool of speculation capital like a shot of adrenaline. Hundreds of applications and petitions poured into Congress from state legislatures, territorial legislatures, and individual corporations (scores of which were constructed of nothing more substantial than pneumatic hopes and simple greed). Congress, sensitive to the needs of the country and generous by instinct (and never mind the number of representatives and senators who, quite incidentally, had contributed personally to the incorporation of sundry railroad companies), was accommodating, to say the least. Between 1850 and 1860, 21 million acres of the public domain were granted to ten public-land states (Florida, Alabama, Louisiana, Mississippi, Michigan, Wisconsin, Iowa, Minnesota, Missouri, and Arkansas) for the intended use of some fifty individual railroad companies.

These corporations, most of which never operated a train, or never finished laying track, or never laid any track, or never got further toward reality than plans drawn up in someone's basement, were less interested in transportation than in jobbery. "This is not a railroad company," a British visitor remarked of the Illinois Central in 1856, "*it is a land company*." The Illinois Central did lay track and operate trains, but its prime concern for many years was suggested by one of its founders, Robert Rantoul, Jr., in 1852: "It is plain that all the land within fifteen miles of the Central Railroad is intrinsically worth, from its power of production, not only as much, but on average twice as high as that which we have assumed to be the selling price of Ohio lands. Such an average would be realized if the supply of such lands were not much greater than the demand for cultivation. It becomes then necessary to inquire how long will the supply exceed the demand . . . ?" Rantoul died before seeing the answer to his question. Illinois grew so fast that demand soon exceeded supply, and the Illinois Central found itself in the happy condition of a seller's market. Between 1854 and 1857 more than half of its grant had been sold for a sum exceeding $15 million at an average of $13.00 per acre. It was a success story whose lesson was not lost on the moneyed and hoped-to-become-moneyed men of the country, and until the end of the Civil War the Mississippi Valley clamored with railroad speculation, so much so that as early as December 3, 1853, President Franklin Pierce felt compelled to voice a gentle rebuke in his Annual Message: "Can it be doubted that the tendency is to run to excess in this matter? Is it wise to augment this excess by encouraging hopes of sudden wealth expected to flow from magnificent schemes dependent upon the action of Congress? . . . It is manifest that, with the most effective guards, there is danger of going too fast and too far."

Too fast? Too far? Such terms were not in the boomer's lexicon, and out of the marriage between land and rails in the Mississippi Valley of the 1850s was born, by Caesarian section, the single greatest land boondoggle in American history—and one of the greatest engineering adventures in the history of the world.

It was not a new idea—for its time, in fact, it was quite an old idea. In the early 1830s, when the vision of a continental America was still as vague as smoke and the railroad industry was still in its infancy, Eastern newspaper editors, filled with the gaseous certitudes characteristic of the breed, were wont to call upon Congress for the creation of a Pacific railroad. Probably such proposals were no more seriously intended than they were received; it was an appealing way to fill editorial space, being devoid of controversy and replete with assurances of America's present and potential greatness; and, of course, newspaper editors have never been required by law to explain precisely *how* their prescriptions might be translated into reality.

But in 1843 a man stepped forward to explain how it might be made to work. His name was Asa Whitney, a New York merchant who had a strong interest in the China trade and a conviction that a Pacific railroad would provide the ideal link to all those millions of

Chinese. His scheme, put before Congress, was that a railroad be constructed from Lake Michigan to the mouth of the Columbia River and that Congress should grant to its builder a strip of public domain sixty miles wide along the whole route. He was only a little ahead of his time, but Congress nonetheless did not act on his proposal, and Whitney took to the stump, lecturing, writing, and petitioning for his idea over the next ten years.

Whether moved by Whitney's proselytizing or by the sheer inevitability of the whole thing, Congress was soon giving the idea of a transcontinental railroad serious consideration. Throughout the 1850s, however, the intensifying sectional rivalry between North and South utterly hamstrung Congress on the question of an appropriate route for such a railroad, and the only concrete result was an authorization in 1853 to have army engineers survey all practical routes between the Mississippi Valley and the Pacific. The ten-volume army study, *Pacific Railroad Reports*, was published in 1855 and outlined not merely two, but *four* feasible routes, two in the North and two in the South—a conclusion that did little to relieve sectional bitterness; in fact, it amplified the opportunity for debate.

With the secession of the Southern states and the outbreak of the Civil War in 1861, debate on the North-South routes ended, yet Congress still might not have moved on the question of a Pacific railroad for several more years had it not been for the artful prodding of Theodore Dehone Judah, a brilliant young engineer. After a precocious career in the East, during which he helped to reconstruct portions of the Erie Canal and built bridges and railroads, Judah was called to California in 1854 to build that state's first railroad, a twenty-five-mile line outside Sacramento, and while there he found the definition of his life in an obsession with the idea of a transcontinental railroad; he wanted, in fact, to build it. With his own money, Judah financed survey trips to determine the best route across the Sierra Nevada and spent most of the rest of his time trying to drum up support for the idea in California. In 1859 the state legislature approved a Pacific Railroad Convention, which met in San Francisco and appointed Judah its official spokesman in Washington, D.C. While sectional problems blocked any significant progress that year, Judah took advantage of the experience to become one of the shrewdest of the mob of lobbyists who prowled the halls of Congress like beggars in Bedlam.

Back in California in 1860, the determined engineer made yet another survey and continued to scout around for financial support. One of those who attended a lecture Judah gave in Sacramento was a local hardware dealer named Collis P. Huntington, a man with a sharply honed instinct for moneyed possibilities. Also in attendance were Huntington's partner, Mark Hopkins, and an associate by the name of Charles Crocker, a recently elected state assemblyman. Huntington listened closely that night; he then invited Judah to come to his home and talk some more. Calculating to the point of bloodlessness, Huntington in his own way was a kind of romantic, and Judah's proposal excited his imagination. He threw his considerable influence behind the project, ultimately convincing Hopkins, Crocker, and another associate, grocer Leland Stanford, to join with him. This quartet would soon and forever after be known as the Big Four. The needed money (amounting to about $1,500 per man) was put together, and on June 28, 1861, the Central Pacific Railroad of California was officially incorporated, with Stanford as president, Huntington as vice-president, Hopkins as treasurer, Judah as chief engineer, and Crocker as construction superintendant.

Reinforced by a workable route, an organization, and the opportunity provided by the Civil War, Judah once again assailed Congress in the summer of 1861 with the occasional aid of Huntington. After months of haggling, feuding, wheeling and dealing—principally with and among various Mississippi Valley railroads struggling to obtain the privilege of building the eastern leg of the transcontinental line—a Pacific Railroad Bill was pried out of Congress on May 7, 1862, and signed by President Lincoln on July 3. Largely drafted by Judah, who had been privileged to sit in on both the House and Senate railroad committees as advisor, the bill divided the responsibility for construction between the Central Pacific and the still-to-be-formed Union Pacific railroads (the C.P. to start east from Sacramento, the U.P. west from Omaha, the two lines to join at some point to be determined by the President at a later date). But the provisions that undoubtedly most stirred the hearts and minds of the Sacramento associates were those regarding federal subsidies. Each railroad would receive the standard right-of-way and the right to use timber and stone from the public domain free of charge, and in addition would be granted alternate sections of the public domain in ten-mile-wide strips on either side of the line, amounting to twenty square miles for every mile of track laid. Finally, they would receive government loans in the form of thirty-year, 6-percent bonds in amounts ranging from $16,000 a mile for construction over flat terrain up to $48,000 a mile for construction over mountainous terrain. A jubilant Huntington wired a five-word message to Stanford in California: "We have drawn the elephant."

THE CURSE OF CALIFORNIA.

Enriched by federal loans and federal land grants, the
Southern Pacific Railroad created a monopoly called an octopus.

So they had—or at least half an elephant. The other half was snapped up finally by Eastern financiers Thomas C. Durant and Sidney Dillon, among others, who put together the organization that assumed the name, the responsibilities, and the land grant of the Union Pacific Railroad. Obeying the biblical injunction that "every mountain shall be made low," the Central Pacific began construction on January 9, 1863 in Sacramento. "The skies smiled yesterday upon a ceremony of vast significance," a reporter for the Sacramento *Union* wrote. "With rites appropriate to the occasion . . . ground was formally broken at noon for the commencement of the Central Pacific Railroad—the California link of the continental chain that is to unite American communities now divided by thousands of miles of trackless wilderness. The muscle, the gold, and the iron were ready to make the railroad a reality." (The muscle, the gold, and the iron—but not Theodore Judah. He had already quarrelled with the Big Four and later that year journeyed to New York via the Isthmus of Panama to get enough financing to buy the rest out, contracted cholera en route, and died.)

On December 2, 1862, the Union Pacific began construction at Omaha, and a little over five years later was under full steam. "It is a grand Anvil Chorus that those sturdy sledges are playing across the plains," wrote an Englishman. "It is in triple time, three strokes to a spike. There are ten spikes to a rail, four hundred rails to a mile, eighteen hundred miles to San Francisco. . . . Twenty-one million times are those sledges to be swung—twenty-one million times are they to come down with their sharp punctuation, before the great work of modern America is complete!"

And then it was done. By May of 1869 both lines had reached the high desert of northern Utah and threatened to pass each other, building off into the distance and collecting their federal subsidies all the way. President Ulysses S. Grant promptly assigned a meeting point at a place called Promontory, and on May 9, 1869, "with rites appropriate to the occasion," the rails of East and West were joined. The nation erupted in a spectral binge of self-congratulation. Unlike the ending of the Civil War four years before, shadowed by the memory of six hundred thousand dead and one assassinated president, the completion of the transcontinental railroad was an event that could be memorialized with enthusiasm and gusto. San Franciscans danced in streets made aromatic by free-flowing whiskey; Mormons gathered in the Great Tabernacle of Salt Lake City to lift paeans to a foresightful Providence; New Yorkers, Philadelphians, and Chicagoans rejoiced, and even Bostonians abandoned their composure. The transcontinental railroad was a national dream, a national pride, and a national experience.

It was also a national disgrace, according to some. "While fighting to retain eleven refractory states," one critic of the day wrote, "the nation permits itself to be cozened out of territory sufficient to form twelve new republics." Perhaps not twelve new republics, but certainly a few good-sized provinces: the grant for the two branches of the transcontinental railroad alone amounted to almost 19 million acres—11,935,121 to the Union Pacific and 6,891,404 to the Central Pacific. In later years, both railroads enlarged their holdings by building branch lines and absorbing other railroads with land-grant property, until the Union Pacific had swelled its grant lands to 19,000,112 acres and the Central Pacific (incorporated into the Southern Pacific Railway Company in 1884) to 20,501,943.

Nor did Congress stop with the Central Pacific and Union Pacific. Caught up in a full-blown infatuation with transcontinental railroads, it granted land and subsidy charters to three more in quick succession: the Northern Pacific (38,916,338 acres), constructed from Lake Superior to Portland, Oregon; the Santa Fe (9,878,352 acres), from Atchison, Kansas to San Bernardino and San Diego, California; and the Southern Pacific (7,444,000 acres), from New Orleans to Yuma, Arizona, and from Yuma to Oakland and San Francisco—owned and operated by the same Big Four who had created the Central Pacific. Smaller grants were also given to a few less ambitious railroads, among them the Burlington & Missouri River, Oregon Central, and Sioux City & Pacific. Altogether, the government granted 91,239,389 acres to Western railroads, and of this total 88,296,745 acres were given to only four corporations—the Union Pacific, Southern Pacific (Central Pacific), Northern Pacific, and the Santa Fe.

The men who owned these corporations—and through them nearly 90 million acres of the national inheritance—were both product and reflection of the complex and frequently brutal drives that characterized America as it developed an industrial civilization. Like Darwinian mutants, they quite literally believed in the rule of tooth and claw, in a jungle morality that recognized no ethic but the ethic of opportunity. Historian David Lavender has described them well in *The Great Persuader*, his biography of Collis P. Huntington: "Self-defense and the survival of the fittest, their attitudes proclaimed, were the first law of economics as well as of nature. In fulfillment of that law they would do, with no sense of wrong, whatever was necessary to protect their great achievement against erosion by politicians, competitors, or raiding speculators, just as they would have protected their homes against robbers or

OVERLEAF: The Union Pacific at the Green River, Wyoming, in the winter of 1868. Citadel Rock in the background.

wild animals. If this involved breaking unjust laws (and the associates could define justice to suit themselves), then they would do it.''

And do it they did. The directors of the Union Pacific, casting about for some quick-money scheme, hit upon the notion of organizing their own construction company, ostensibly independent of the railroad company, to build the railroad west to Promontory and in the process siphon off so much of the federal loans that the railroad itself was kept in a state of near bankruptcy while the officers of the construction company—the Credit Mobilier, it was called, after a convenient French example—raked in a profit that has been estimated at somewhere between $33 million and $50 million. Unfortunately, they spread a little too much money around among the members of Congress "where it would do the most good," and the resulting scandal gave America a pre-Watergate taste of corruption. The associates of the Central Pacific, no sluggards in such matters, formed their own construction company, too, the Contract Finance Corporation, charging their own railroad an estimated $120 million for the construction of a line that had in reality cost less than $58 million. It should be said, however, that Collis P. Huntington was much too shrewd to be caught in the act of passing bribes unless they were absolutely necessary, and on the national level he did not normally find it necessary.

California was a different matter entirely, for an empire was at stake. Under Huntington's careful, patient supervision, the Central Pacific gathered unto itself a total of nine individual state railroads (which is to say all the railroads in the state worth a major corporation's interest), reincorporated into the Southern Pacific Railway Company in 1884, and proceeded to run its railroad how, when, where, and for how much it chose. To ensure that its stranglehold on the state's transportation economy would not be meddled with in any significant fashion, Huntington methodically bought politicians at both state and local levels, either through outright gifts or promises of financial and arm-twisting help during elections—and the corollary threat of powerful opposition. It would be a full generation before the grip of "The Octopus" would be broken, and even today it remains a major force in the state, not only in transportation but as a landholder; the Southern Pacific still owns 2,411,000 acres, making it the single largest private landowner in California.

Hastened to its demise by the acts and attitudes of the Huntingtons, the Durants, and the Stanfords, the age of federal land grants to railroads ended even more quickly than it had begun. In the

December 1870 issue of the *Nation*—barely a year-and-a-half after the golden spike had been driven at Promontory, Utah—J.B. Hodgkin noted: "It is only within the last few years that a doubt has risen in the public mind as to whether, after all, the policy of giving away the lands almost indiscriminately to great railroad corporations is wise as we thought it to be ten years ago. In the West, especially, this doubt has almost developed into positive opposition, and . . . many leading men in both Houses of Congress, as well as President Grant, have openly expressed their downright hostility to the present system." All of the party platforms during the 1872 elections condemned the system, and the Democratic Party in 1874 demanded outright "reform to stop waste of public lands. . . . "

America, it seemed, had looked around and found that hundreds of millions of acres of the public domain had disappeared in less than a century—sold, stolen, given away, gone. And with them, it was feared, had gone the noblest hope the land had ever held for Americans. "It needs no reference to census tables or special facts," Henry George wrote in 1886, "to prove that under present conditions the small American freeholder is doomed. . . . We are on the verge of an event which is, in some respects, the most important that has occurred since Columbus sighted land—the 'fencing in' of the last available quarter section of the American domain."

V

ACTION, REACTION, AND REVOLUTION

NOTES ON THE GILDED AGE: in 1870 Senator James W. Grimes of Iowa penned a despondent letter to his fellow Republican, Senator Lyman Trumbull of Illinois, declaring that the Grand Old Party was no longer so grand as it was old, that it had "gone to the dogs" and had further become "the most corrupt and debauched political party that has ever existed." In 1872 Henry Wadsworth Longfellow, the kindly optimist-poet who had given "Hiawatha" and "The Courtship of Myles Standish" to American literature—or at least to American verse—looked about him at the state of the Union and was driven to something resembling bitterness:

> Ah, woe is me!
> I hoped to see my country rise to heights
> Of happiness and freedom yet unreached
> By other nations, but the climbing wave
> Pauses, lets go its hold, and slides again
> Back to the common level, with a hoarse
> Death-rattle in its throat. I am too old
> To hope for better days.

Poet and politician both had reason enough for despair. The period from about 1870 to the end of the century saw the forces of corruption riddle the processes of government like borers turned loose in a field of Kansas corn. In California the Southern Pacific Railroad bought legislators as if they were maidens on an Arabian auction block; in New York the "Tweed Ring" siphoned off city and state tax money as neatly as a mink sucking eggs. Jay Gould, Jim Fisk, and sundry officials in the Department of the Treasury conspired to engineer the greenback swindle of 1869, which in the words of Henry Adams, "smirched executive, judiciary, banks,

87

Major John Wesley Powell, the one-armed practical idealist
who saw the land for what it was—and what it could be.

corporate systems, professions, and people, all the great active forces of society." In Congress, the Credit Mobilier spread bribes around like litter in a public park. In the Executive Branch, a "Whiskey Ring" scandal reached into the Oval Office to touch President Grant's personal secretary, General Orville E. Babcock. In the War Department the Secretary of War was discovered to have accepted a $25,000 kickback from an Indian post trader he had appointed, and more than a million board feet of lumber vanished from the Boston navy yard, never to be seen again.

It was a catalogue of political horrors documenting one of the least enlightened epochs in American history. But the law of action and reaction can be applied to the social world as well as the physical world, and this same period witnessed the restless stirring of reform. "Mugwump" Republicans, disgusted at the condition of their party, forced the election in 1884 of Democrat Grover Cleveland, a dour, troubled man of granitic integrity; "We love him for the enemies he has made," the Mugwumps said. In the 1890s Populism stirred democracy's pot, finding its voice—and such a voice!—in the Great Commoner, William Jennings Bryan. And shortly after the turn of the century, Progressivism tasted power in the leadership of Theodore Roosevelt, a man made president in 1901 by the bullets of an assassin, but reelected in 1904 by the force of an idea.

Of the major reforms effected by the various and sometimes conflicting strands of this movement—civil service, direct election of senators, antitrust legislation, initiative, referendum, and recall—none was more charged with passion, more dramatic, more bitterly opposed, and more far-reaching in importance than the revision of the national land system. It could hardly have been otherwise, for the implementation of its goals—conservation instead of waste, management instead of exploitation— was a head-on challenge to the tenacity of myth and the inflexibility of tradition. It was a revolution, in fact; a revolution in ideas, a long, painful revolution that has continued to our own day, a revolution whose battle lines were drawn just as clearly as if they had been sketched on some military map. Listen to two men, each speaking in 1910—first, Gifford Pinchot, Chief Forester of the United States, who believed that the foremost duty of the country was to "bring about a fundamental change in the law and the practice toward conservation, to prevent for the future what has been in the past, the useless sacrifice of the public welfare, and to make possible hereafter the utilization of the natural resources and the natural advantages for the benefit of all the people instead of merely for the profit of a few"; now, Thomas Burke, senator from the state of Washington: "The people of today have a right to share in the blessings of nature. There is no intention in the West to rob the future, but there is a determined purpose not to let a band of well-meaning sentimentalists rob the present on the plea that it is necessary to hoard Nature's riches for unborn generations."

The revolution was already more than thirty years old when they spoke. They could have been speaking today, which might lead one to question the theory that man is a learning animal.

This revolution began at perhaps the lowest point in the history of the public domain, a time when lumbermen, stockmen, and speculators were perverting the various land laws without notable interference from the government, when railroad men were enjoying the fruits of the incredible gift of land Congress in its wisdom had bestowed upon them, when the luckless homesteader, pinched and worried, was doggedly illustrating the dictum of Senator William E. Borah that "The government bets 160 acres against the entry fee . . . that the settler can't live on the land for five years without starving to death."

It began, largely, and certainly in its single most revolutionary form, as an expression of the mind and vision of Major John Wesley Powell, director of the Powell Survey of the Plateau Province of the Colorado River. Essentially self-educated, the one-armed major (his right arm had been contributed to the cause of the Union at the battle of Shiloh) had by 1878 established himself as one of the leading scientific men of his generation. His Rocky Mountain Exploring Expedition of 1866 to 1867 had given that region its first major scientific examination; his Colorado River Exploring Expeditions of 1869 and 1872 had illuminated the spectacular geology of the Grand Canyon as never before and had produced a book that remains a literal classic of science/adventure, *Exploration of the Colorado River of the West*; and his survey of the Plateau Province, detailed, methodical, and comprehensive, had gone a long way toward cataloguing the resources of one of the largest geographic regions of the arid West. But Powell was more than explorer, more than field scientist, more even than a conscientious public servant in an age that more often than not looked upon government service as a handy path to the hog trough of federal money. He was that singularly American phenomenon, a practical idealist, a sober visionary who believed—and believed that he could prove it— that by the application of energy, information, and common sense men

could transform the present and shape the future, creating a world he described in a speech before the Anthropological Society in 1878, a world where "the enmity of man to man is appeased, and men live and labor for one another," where "individualism is transmuted into socialism, egoism into altruism, and man is lifted above the brute to an immeasurable height." To such a man, the data being painstakingly compiled by his massive survey were something more than the necessary accumulation of facts; they were the pieces in the puzzle of an idea.

Powell first presented that idea in 1878 with the publication of his *Report on the Lands of the Arid Region of the United States*, an innocuously titled volume whose message was nothing less than a frontal assault on the shibboleths of a century. First, he noted that in the arid West an unirrigated 160-acre farm was incapable of supporting a homesteader and his family (thousands of defeated farmers would have been happy to testify to that), but with water it blossomed so splendidly that a single family simply could not cope with it; therefore, he recommended that the size of an irrigated homestead be reduced to 80 acres. Second, he pointed out that the nature of pasturage in the West required far more than 160 acres —or even the 640 acres available under the Desert Land Act—of grazing land to feed enough cattle to support a family; therefore, he proposed that grazing land be carved into blocks of 2,560 acres, sixteen times the homestead unit. Third, he explained that the traditional Western approach to water use—simple appropriation—inevitably tended toward the monopolization of land, since he who claimed and held an upstream "right" to water effectively controlled the land for miles below and around it; therefore, Powell suggested that all homestead or pasturage units offered for settlement be vested with equal rights to available water, and to accomplish this recommended that the ninety-three-year-old system of rectangular surveys be abandoned so that streamside land units could be fashioned as irregularly as was necessary to provide each with a water frontage.

Already Powell had done violence to tradition, but he was not finished. Since privately fenced grazing land was demonstrably vulnerable to overgrazing and too often trapped cattle as they drifted before the pressure of winter storms (as would happen in 1886 to 1887 on a scale never before seen), he advocated the elimination of fencing to restore the open range and to prevent the water-controlled land monopoly that even as he wrote was becoming characteristic of the open-range West. He suggested that the government actively encourage the formation of cooperative organiza-

Butte near Florence Creek in Desolation Canyon—a part of John Wesley Powell's public domain.

tions that would own and control pasturage lands in common, as the Spanish and Mexican towns of New Mexico had done for nearly two centuries. Similarily, it was obvious to Powell that individual farmers would be incapable of financing the major irrigation necessary to nourish their land in the arid region, and he consequently suggested that the government either encourage the creation of cooperative irrigation districts whose common financing might be able to build the needed dams and ditches, or simply step in itself to control and distribute the water.

"Bolshevism" was not yet a cant epithet utilized by the mossbacks of the nation, but if it had been, it is certain that this word would have been used to describe Powell's proposals when they became public. As it was, among the mildest of the outraged responses that greeted his report—most of them coming from Western interests—was a description of Powell himself as "a charlatan in science and intermeddler in affairs of which he has no proper conception." In truth, Powell's concept, so sensible, so reasonable, so *workable*, was so far ahead of its time that, as Bernard DeVoto wrote nearly seventy-five years later, "we are still far short of catching up with it," and in the context of the last quarter of the nineteenth century was no more likely to be implemented than a proposal, say, to turn over the Union Pacific Railroad to the federal government for operation.

Powell tried. In June, 1878, the prestigious National Academy of Sciences was assigned by Congress the task of giving advice on what should be done with the various Western surveys (Powell's Plateau Province survey was only one of many). Through the cooperation of the reform-minded Secretary of the Interior, Carl Schurz, Powell was not only kept informed of the Academy's deliberations on the subject, but was enabled to influence them—to what degree we do not know, but it is suggestive to note that when the Academy made its recommendations to Congress in November, they included the consolidation of the Western surveys (which Powell had advocated), the revision of land-parceling surveys (which Powell had advocated), and the creation of a public lands commission to examine land laws with an eye toward changing and rationalizing them (which Powell had most definitely advocated). At Schurz's request, Powell then drafted bills that incorporated the Academy's suggestions, and early in 1879 they were introduced in Congress as riders to various appropriations bills (a deliberate and successful device calculated to keep them out of the antedeluvian public lands committees of both houses of Congress).

Opposition was immediate and violent. Most of it, predictably

Gray Canyon of the Green River; it was through here that "The Major" floated on his way to the greater canyons of the Colorado river in 1869 and 1872.

enough, came from Western senators and congressmen fully committed to the representation of myth and of those interests that had
learned to use it to their advantage. Powell's bills (and it was well
known that he had authored them) denied myth and threatened
those who used it; when the House was through with them, however, he had won two out of three: the creation of the U.S. Geological Survey, and the authorization of a Public Lands Commission. In
the heavily Republican Senate, it was another matter. One newly
introduced amendment simply eliminated the entire proposal, and
only determined in-fighting on the part of those who supported it
managed to reconstruct the legislation to the form in which it had
passed the House. In that form it was passed by the Senate and
signed into law by President Rutherford B. Hayes in March 1879.
Clarence King was subsequently appointed director of the U.S.
Geological Survey, and the Public Lands Commission was headed
by him and Commissioner of the General Land Office, together
with a number of presidential appointees (among them, John Wesley Powell).

In 1880, the Public Lands Commission issued its report, a
bulky, detailed, and comprehensive (if not consistently accurate)
document compiled by Thomas Donaldson. Perhaps its greatest
contribution was the first codification of all the laws, acts, ordinances, amendments, rules, regulations, revisions, and orders
(more than three thousand of them) that had been applied to the
public domain since 1785, but one of its conclusions might have
been written by Powell himself. The "most conspicuous characteristic" of the West, it said, "is its heterogeneity. One region is
exclusively valuable for mining, another solely for timber, a third
for nothing but pasturage, and a fourth serves no useful purpose
whatever. . . . Hence it has come to pass that the homestead and
preemption laws are not suited for securing the settlement of more
than an insignificant portion of the country." It also recommended
that the land be classified according to its mineral, timber, grazing,
and irrigation resources.

The report of the Commission was promptly printed by the
Government Printing Office, distributed to Congress, and—as
Powell and his colleagues had known it would be—was swiftly
ignored. Powell was neither deterred nor discouraged. The report
was there, at least. In 1881, he succeeded Clarence King as head of
the Geological Survey and began the long, painstaking task of providing the United States with its first official, complete, and accurate topographical map (the job is not yet finished). In 1888, that
duty was significantly expanded, not at Powell's instigation but

with his enthusiastic approval. In that year, Senator William ("Big Bill") Stewart of Nevada introduced a resolution in Congress asking the Secretary of the Interior to investigate the possibility of having the Geological Survey designate irrigable lands and reservoir and canal sites in the arid region. The Secretary passed along the inquiry to Powell. The Major was willing—so willing that he joined in an unlikely alliance with Stewart to engineer a Joint Resolution through Congress that directed the Department of the Interior to initiate a study of irrigation possibilities in the West. During the appropriation effort that followed, Representative George Symes of Colorado threw in an antispeculation amendment that would remove from settlement all lands "susceptible of irrigation," thus abrogating for a major part of the remaining public domain all existing land laws. In response to the howls of protest, Stewart in the Senate introduced a second amendment that would empower the President to reopen any reserved lands to settlement at his discretion, but only under the provisions of the Homestead Act.

The compromise passed and Powell began his irrigation study. Stewart, who wished the classification to be done as quickly as possible so that development could follow swiftly upon its heels, observed Powell's progress at first with enthusiasm, then with puzzlement, then with impatience, and finally with anger. He had not counted on Powell's care, his precision, his dedication to thoroughness. Most of all, he had not counted on the Major's larger purpose—if he even understood what that was. For Powell was not interested in quickly setting aside lands that Stewart and his colleagues could just as quickly exploit. He saw the irrigation survey as an opportunity to implement the spirit—and hopefully the recommendations—of his *Arid Regions* report, to rationalize for the first time and with the tools of science America's century-old land system. He would not be hurried. And while he did not hurry, the lands were closed.

The inevitable conflict broke when Powell made his standard appropriation request to Congress in the spring of 1890, and Stewart was in the thick of it. After a spring, summer, and fall of hearings and debate, Powell's vision was finally punctured and deflated; by act of Congress the reservation of all public domain lands was cancelled, entries on that land made in "good faith" after their closure in 1888 were declared valid, Powell's $720,000 budget request for the irrigation survey was reduced to $162,500, and no mention was made in the language of the legislation of hydrographic work—which amounted to a repudiation of the act of 1888 that had ordered it done. Two years later, Stewart and his cohorts had at Powell again, this time gutting the Geological Survey itself, reducing its budget by $90,000 and eliminating sixteen staff positions. Powell decided he had beaten his head against the wall long enough; in 1894 he retired from the Survey and devoted his energies to the Bureau of American Ethnology, which he had created in 1879. The Major was out of the land business.

Powell died in 1902, a matter of weeks after Congress had given at least part of his vision reality—without his guidance, without his strength—by passage of the Newlands Act, which created the Reclamation Service and put the federal government to work for the first time as a dam, canal, and waterworks builder. One provision in the act would have satisfied him, for it stipulated that water delivered from federally built irrigation projects would be limited to parcels of 160 acres or less (or 320 acres for an average family), and that any landowner holding more than that was by law required to sell his excess lands within ten years after signing an entitlement contract with the government for water. The Major would not have been pleased, however, to learn that the 160-acre limitation—designed to end land-water monopoly in the West forever—was not consistently enforced in the years immediately following creation of the Reclamation Service, was not consistently enforced in 1923 when the agency became the Bureau of Reclamation, was not consistently enforced when the Bureau proceeded to inflict concrete on nearly every river and river system in the West, and is not consistently enforced today.

Powell's genius was also his weakness. His vision was too large for his time to contain, although its assumptions exerted a measurable influence on the thinking of that time—and of our own, for that matter. It was left to men with smaller, more fragmented perceptions to institute the changes that survived the power plays of reaction. Reform came gradually, it came piecemeal, it came too often hampered by the right-hand-does-not-know-what-the-left-hand-is-doing syndrome, it came without the sense of program that would have given it cohesion. But it came, and if the men who brought it lacked Powell's largeness of purpose, they lacked nothing of his passion.

Consider William Andrew Jackson Sparks, appointed Land Commissioner by President Grover Cleveland in the spring of 1885. Unlike Powell, Sparks was devoid of tact, charm, or humor, but he did possess conviction. Poring over his predecessor's thick files on the popular abuse of the various land laws, particularly that perpe-

Water, land, and people: Above, a farmer cuts a slice out of a dike and Reclamation Service water irrigates his farm in California's Imperial Valley, 1905; below, a modern automated sprinkler spews water from the California Aquaduct.

trated under the provisions of the Timber and Stone act of 1878 (see Chapter 3), Sparks was appalled. "I was confronted," he wrote in his first annual report, "with overwhelming evidence that the public domain was being made the prey of unscrupulous speculation and the worst forms of land monopoly through systematic frauds carried on and consummated under the public land laws. . . . Reports of special agents, registers and receivers, and inspectors of surveyors-general and local land offices, communications from United States attorneys and other officials, and letters from public men and private citizens throughout the country, were laid before me, all detailing one common story of widespread, persistent land robbery committed under guise of the various forms of public land entry."

His solution was as simple as it was direct. He suspended from final action all entries made in those areas where major frauds had been detected, including all of Colorado except the Ute Indian Reservation, all of Wyoming, Idaho, Dakota Territory, Utah, Washington, and New Mexico, and large parts of Kansas, Nebraska, and Minnesota. That done, he sent special agents into the field to investigate as many suspected frauds as possible. Furthermore, Sparks began agitating out loud for the elimination of cash sales of public lands, the substitution of fixed salaries instead of commission payments for land agents (under the present system, he noted, such agents were more interested in getting claims settled than in finding out if they were fraudulent), and the outright abolition of the Pre-emption Act, the Timber and Stone Act, the Desert Land Act, and the commutation provision of the Homestead Act.

This was reform by administrative fiat; it was an act more of courage than of good sense, and it did not last. Responding to the pressure from a small army of Western interests (as well as Eastern financiers with more than a small stake in the continuation of the system), the Secretary of the Interior summarily dismissed Sparks in November, 1887, and in the spring of the following year revoked his entire program—but not before it had restored an estimated 80 million acres of public domain that had been illegally claimed.

Sparks was singular, but not alone. The revulsion over the continuing subversion of the land laws—and particularly over the manner in which so much of the public domain had become the satrapy of such corporate interests as railroads—had not swelled to the dimensions of Longfellow's "climbing wave" by the middle of the 1880s, but it could be called a wavelet, at least, and it held the distinct promise of becoming something more. In 1885, President Cleveland ordered Western stockmen to cease and desist their practice of sealing off tracts of the public domain with barbed wire, a method designed not only to keep one another's cattle and sheep from mingling but to effectively wall off such land from homestead settlement. In that same year, Congress considered legislation to repeal the Pre-emption Act; it passed the Senate, but was defeated in the House. In 1886, an act was introduced that called for the abolition of the Pre-emption Act, the Timber Culture Act, and the Desert Land Act, and for a revision of the Homestead Act; it passed both houses, but a bicameral squabble over amendments sent the bill to a conference committee, where it expired in the spring of 1887. The year 1888 saw the Joint Resolution that ordered the Geological Survey to investigate irrigation sites. Finally, early in 1890 yet another reform attempt was introduced; this one again passed both houses easily enough and again was sent into conference committee to iron out amendments—but this time it was reported out of committee, approved by the House, and sent to President Benjamin Harrison, who signed it into law on March 3, 1891.

The General Revision Act of 1891 planted the seeds for the revolution's first healthy sprout, although one had to search among its nearly thirty sections to find them. The act repealed the Pre-emption Act, the Timber Culture Act, and the auction sale of land, but it left the Timber and Stone Act untouched and did not provide—as many insisted it should—for the classification of the public lands. It reduced the acreage limitation under the Desert Land Act from 640 to 320 acres and amended the Homestead Act to the effect that no commutation of title could take place until fourteen months after the filing of a claim, but these actions were, as one historian has written, cases of having "locked the barndoor after the horse was stolen." Section 24 of the act was another matter entirely. Later called the Forest Reserve Act, it authorized the President of the United States to withdraw from settlement or exploitation any forest areas of the public domain which in his opinion required watershed protection and timber preservation, such reserves to be administered under the supervision of the Department of the Interior.

This idea, tacked on to the General Revision bill during its consideration in the Senate, did not spring full-grown from some senatorial brow. It was the first legislative expression of a concept that had been growing in importance ever since the Civil War. We speak of it today, somewhat condescendingly, as "utilitarian conservation," but "protective custody" might be an equally apt description, for those who voiced it—forestry associations, scientific groups, and each of the several Land Commissioners after 1877—pointed to the record of unregulated forest use all over the West, the denuded hillsides and mountainsides, the land slippage that had clogged and diverted streams, the annual floods that sent a juggernaut of mud and rock into towns and over farms, the erosion that was reducing much of the land to a moonscape, and declared that unrestrained corporate and individual enterprise was not simply cheating the land laws but destroying the future. Not even Congress could ignore destruction so obvious, particularly when its awareness was pricked with increasing persistence by alarmed petitioners from inside and outside the government during the 1880s. Moreover, there was precedent for such reserves, for in 1872 Yellowstone National Park—the first such—had been established in Wyoming, and in 1890 Sequoia, General Grant (later merged with Sequoia), and Yosemite national parks had been created in California (such withdrawals would continue; between 1890 and 1921 thirteen additional parks would be established).

The precedent was there and the need was so obvious that the West hardly whimpered when President Harrison proceeded to create by executive order fifteen major reservations between 1891 and 1893. In truth, it must be noted that at least one of the reasons for the region's uncharacteristically docile response was the active support the reserve system received from the corporate lumber industry—inspired less by any altruistic or ecological motive than by an interest in protecting the timber monopolies they had so methodically assembled by a judicious use of the homestead, pre-emption, and timber laws. In any case, the honeymoon, if such it could be called, did not last long, for in 1896, the last year of the second administration of Grover Cleveland, the Secretary of the Interior requested the National Academy of Sciences to investigate the "necessity of a radical change in the existing policy with reference to the disposal of and preservation of the forests upon the public domain. . . ." The Academy accommodated the Secretary by sending a committee on a swing through the forested West from July to October. Upon its return, the committee began preparing a report among whose recommendations was the addition of several more reserves, and although the report would not become official until its publication more than six months later, President Cleveland implemented it as one of the last acts of his administration. On Washington's Birthday, 1897, he proclaimed the addition of 21 million acres to the forest system in thirteen individual reserves from the Cascade Range of Washington to the Black Hills of South Dakota. All further land, mining, or timber entries on these reserves were forbidden, and those in existence at the time of the proclamation—pending or final—would be exempted only if they were found to have adhered to the letter of the law (a test thousands of entries could by no means survive). Finally, grazing by sheep and cattle was prohibited.

This was a bit much—more than a bit, in fact. With one stroke of the executive pen, Cleveland had managed to outrage the three major economic powers in the West: the stockmen, the miners, and the timbermen, not to mention the railroad men, much of whose grant land was included in these reserves and therefore rendered unexploitable (the struggling homesteader, whose wizened spectre was invoked repeatedly by these interests to gain sympathy for their cause, remained strangely unmoved by Cleveland's act of "tyranny"). The Western press obediently began the drumroll of opposition. "Every right-minded citizen," the Cheyenne *Tribune* announced, "is heartily in favor of preserving the forests of the state, but it is well known that the segregating of the forest areas under present laws into reserves whose boundary lines are impassable barriers to the settler . . . is a dangerous and ridiculous farce." "A Menace to the Interests of the Western States," headlined the Denver *Republican*, and the editor of the San Francisco *Chronicle* averred that the withdrawals had been made "for no other reason than that the wiseacres of the National Academy of Science, who nominated the amiable theorists who reported a scheme of forest reservations for the West, believed that what would be well for one part of the country would be the best for all."

Answering the call to action, Western representatives in Congress took up their legislative cudgels and went after the program of the wiseacres and amiable theorists who were out to wreck the West. In May 1897, they pushed through an act whose several sections authorized the Secretary of the Interior to make timber and stone on the reserves available to settlers, miners, or other residents for purposes of firewood, fencing, construction, mining, and prospecting; opened the reserves to mining and prospecting; and provided that any individual (or corporation) who possessed a claim under the several land laws in such reserves could relinquish that claim and in lieu of it select an area of the same size on other sections of the unsettled, but surveyed, public domain. In short, without actually repudiating the Forest Reserve Act of 1891 (the idea had gained too much strength by 1897), Western interests managed to cripple its application. As they had hoped and fully expected, the heavily conservative pen of William McKinley approved their legislation within a week after its passage.[3]

OVERLEAF: Armed with axes and the Timber and Stone Act, lumberjacks pose with the centuries they have cut down.

The movement for forest conservation was stunned, but not staggered; like Gene Rhodes' good man who knew he was right, its supporters just shook their heads and kept on coming. In 1898 the embryonic Forestry Department of the Department of the Interior was pieced together under the leadership of Chief Forester Gifford Pinchot, who had served as a member of the Academy of Science's 1896 investigating committee. Hamstrung by miniscule appropriations and a stony lack of enthusiasm emanating from the executive, Pinchot functioned in something of a vacuum for two years, but was given reason for hope when McKinley chose Theodore Roosevelt, former civil service commissioner and a certified reformer, as his running mate in his successful bid for reelection in 1900. He was given even more reason for hope on September 6, 1901, when an anarchist madman stepped up to the always available McKinley and pumped a bullet into his stomach.

New York patrician by birth, Western cowboy by avocation, and mover-and-shaker by instinct, Roosevelt proved a ready listener and a vigorous ally of Pinchot's forestry ideas, and his administration—bold, blustery, self-consciously (and frequently self-righteously) progressive—put teeth in the movement for resource management and land reform. That adminstration added more than 100 million acres to the forest reserve system, bringing the total by 1909 to over 150 million in 159 individual forests. It supported Pinchot's drive to make the Forestry Department an agency large and complex and expert enough to administer the forests intelligently, and in 1905 engineered its transfer from the Department of the Interior to the Department of Agriculture, renaming it the United States Forest Service and renaming the reserves the National Forests. It saw the development of a bidding system for the privilege of cutting timber from National Forest lands and a leasing system to allow summer grazing, both of which would, it was hoped, provide for the utilization of resources without exposing them to the wretched excesses of the past.

The adminstration did not confine itself to the question of the National Forests. It had been Roosevelt's support that had helped create the Reclamation Service in 1902, and he spread that support around. In 1902 his Secretary of the Interior, Ethan Allen Hitchcock, launched an investigation into land frauds that returned some 1 million acres to the public domain. In 1903 Roosevelt appointed a new Public Lands Commission to examine "the conditions, operations, and effect of the present land laws, and to recommend such changes as are needed. . . . " In 1904 he backed passage of the Kinkaid Homestead Act, which allowed entries of 640 acres in the Sand Hills region of western Nebraska (only one-

The land appropriated: A few of the hundreds of mining claims in the Cripple Creek District of Colorado, 1900.

fourth the area of pasture land that Powell had called for in 1878, but a step in the right direction; the act was so successful that a demand rose for its extension to the rest of the public-land states). In 1905, following the report of the Public Lands Commission, a "vicious piece of legislation," the Forest Lieu Land Act of 1897 was repealed, and an executive order from the Department of the Interior suspended all entries under the provisions of the Timber and Stone Act of 1878.

In 1906 Roosevelt directed the Secretary of the Interior to withdraw from entry more than 50 million acres of coal lands in the West, previously obtainable through the exercise of the various land laws, and in that same year the Department established the important precedent of leasing, rather than selling outright, sites on the public domain for the development of hydroelectric plants. In 1907 Roosevelt withdrew from entry 85 million acres in the Pacific Northwest and Alaska pending an evaluation of their mineral values by the Geological Survey. In 1908 he organized a National Conservation Commission, chaired by Gifford Pinchot, to survey the problems and prospects of national conservation policy; its three-volume report, the largest since Donaldson's 1883 document, was issued in December of that year and was described by economist-historian John Ise in 1920 as "the most exhaustive inventory of our natural resources that has ever been made." In 1909 Roosevelt expanded the conservation concept beyond the boundaries of the United States by heading the North American Conservation Conference on February 18, shortly before he left office. And finally, like exclamation points scattered through the years of his administration, Roosevelt had created two national game preserves, five national parks, and fifty-one wild bird refuges.

By any measurement it was the nation's single most concentrated effort to coordinate and rationalize the use, disposal, and meaning of the public domain since the Ordinance of 1785. It was not done perfectly, nor by any means completely, but it was done with a momentum and a kind of autocratic enthusiasm that simply confounded the opposition. Only once during his administrations were the anti-conservationists able to slow Roosevelt's bustling, go-ahead charge. Rallying around the annual appropriations bill for the Forest Service in February 1907, they had tacked on an amendment that provided that "Hereafter no forest reserve shall be created, nor shall any addition be made to one heretofore created, within the limits of the States of Oregon, Washington, Idaho, Montana, Colorado, or Wyoming except by act of Congress." The appropriation (for more than $1 million) was passed with the

Not all mining claims were major industries; for example, consider the grubby Coconino Silver Mine of New Mexico, seen here in 1890. This is all it ever was.

amendment intact, but in a Cleveland-like gesture, Roosevelt calmly proclaimed the addition of twenty-one new forest reserves—just hours before he signed the appropriations bill into law.

If Powell had been the revolution's prophet, Roosevelt had been its champion, and his energy had given it muscle and direction, strength enough to survive the inevitable reaction that followed the years of his administration. It withstood the bitter, perpetual, stubborn, and sometimes mindless sniping and harassment of the West, the lukewarm administration of Interior Secretary Richard Ballinger during the presidency of William Howard Taft (which saw the dismissal of Gifford Pinchot as director of the Forest Service), even the frankly hostile administration of Secretary Franklin K. Lane during the presidency of Woodrow Wilson. An idea had been loosed, and while it could be slowed and diverted, it could not be stopped.

The eleven years between 1909 and 1920 saw the passage of the Enlarged Homestead Act of 1909, which increased the claim size from 160 acres to 320, and the Stock-Raising Homestead Act of 1916, which allowed for entry on 640 acres of grazing land. It saw the Withdrawal Act of 1910, which authorized the president to withdraw public lands from entry for any public purpose, and the consequent reservation of 30 million acres of coal lands, 2 million acres of phosphate lands, 5 million acres of oil land, 7.5 million acres of potash lands, 169,000 acres of oil-shale land, 12,000 acres of helium land, and 8,500 acres of land containing other minerals. It saw the Weeks Act of 1911, which authorized the United States to purchase timberland in the Appalachian and White mountains in order to extend the National Forest system into the East. It saw the federal government locked in a seven-year struggle with the Western states over jurisdictional rights to water-power sites, a conflict resolved by the Supreme Court in 1917 (U.S. *vs.* Utah Power & Light Company), the court holding that the United States had the exclusive power to regulate how and when public lands could be acquired or used. And in 1920 the eleven years were climaxed with passage of the General Mineral Leasing Act, which opened reserved mineral lands to leasing, and the Federal Water-Power Act, which created the Federal Power Commission to regulate the development and utilization of power on public-domain sites.

In twenty years the movement for the reservation, management, and protection of the public domain had evolved from a

*Teddy Roosevelt and Gifford Pinchot, Chief Forester, in
full dress and amiable conversation, 1905.*

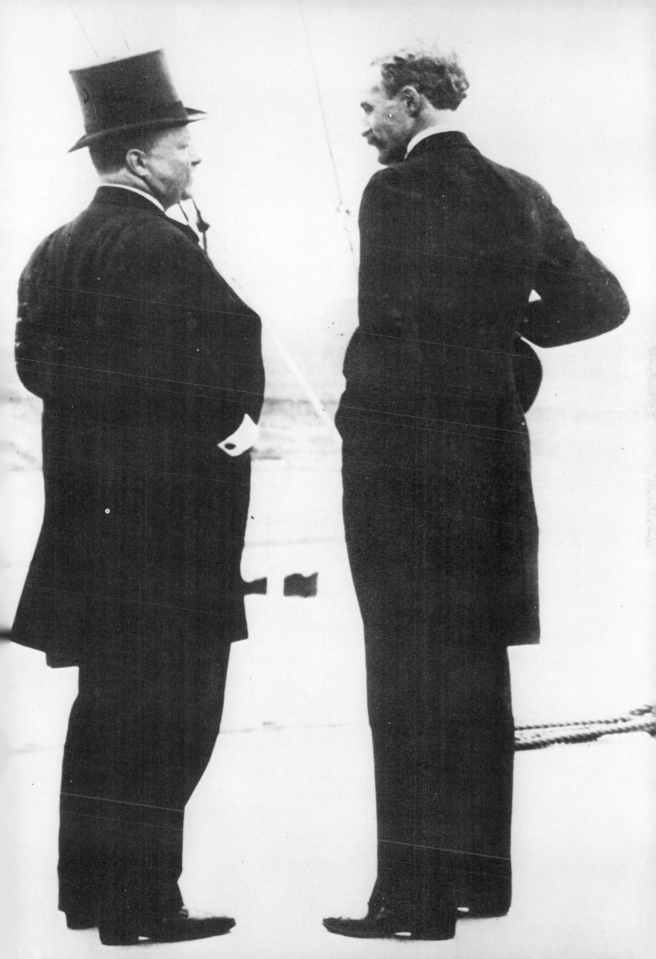

more-than-slightly radical notion to one whose respectability was recognized even by the West (always with certain exceptions, of course, usually having to do with some interest's economic toes getting stepped on by the public good). More than 200 million acres outside Alaska had been rescued from the tyranny of tradition and placed under the mantle of federal retention and administration (for the situation concerning Alaska in these years, see Chapter 7). Yet approximately 190 million acres of unreserved and undisposed land remained, much of it arid or semiarid, little of it understood even forty years after Powell had recommended what to do with it, some of it not even suspected to exist (in 1926 the General Land Office "discovered" more than 11 million acres of unrecorded land, an area more than twice the size of Massachusetts), and all of it virtually ignored during the most exciting and productive period in the history of American conservation. No one in government, no one in the conservation movement, quite simply, had figured out what to *do* with this land, who was to own it, who was to use it and to what purpose. Reclamation law had barely affected it by 1920, and never would affect more than a fraction of it. Homesteading certainly had not worked; it had not worked in 1862 and had not worked after the Enlarged Homestead Act of 1909, or even when the demand for foodstuffs during World War I had sent thousands onto the high plains in an attempt to grow wheat and grow rich, only to grow quite as busted as any dirt farmer of the 1870s.

But there were those who believed they did know what to do with the land, who should own it, to what purpose it should be put—the range industry. As if responding to some physical law, the industry had slipped into the administrative vacuum, planted its feet (or its hooves), and intended to stay put. As it had since the 1870s, this group looked upon the grazing land of the national domain as its own. It wished to use it as it saw fit, without restriction, intervention, or supervision by muddle-headed desk men in Washington (although it had been willing enough to accept the encouragement of those desk men to rebuild the fences that President Cleveland had ordered to come down in the 1880s—this during World War I in an effort to increase meat production for wartime use). The result, predictably enough, was yet another case of widespread overgrazing, and as historian Roy M. Robbins has written, "In the 'twenties, the High Plains of America presented a gloomy spectacle: abandoned homesteads everywhere; grazing lands in very poor condition, some beyond rehabilitation; and more significant still, the big stockmen gradually extending their influence as well as their fences over the public domain."

For all the influence and "rugged individualism" (their ter-
minology) these corporate stockmen possessed, they appeared
peculiarly insecure. Who knew when the Washington bureaucracy
might attempt to regulate their God-given right to use the land?
And what would the oppressed stockman do then? This far into the
twentieth century, a man couldn't hire a gang of thugs to patrol
"his" grazing land, and the shooting of federal rangers probably
would be frowned upon. To forestall— in fact, eliminate—the possiblity of federal interference, the stockmen turned to Congress,
and in 1926 the Stanfield bill was introduced. It was a splendidly
arrogant measure, providing for the division of the public domain's
grazing land into grazing districts, requiring the General Land Office to hand out perpetual contracts to the members of those districts, demanding that all other uses of the land be prohibited,
allowing the grazing contracts to be bought and sold, and further
specifying that the permit system of the National Forests be
abolished and their grazing land turned over to the range industry,
which knew best how to protect it, as it had proved so many times.
Except for those journals sitting more-or-less directly under the
thumb of the industry, the proposed legislation was something not
even Western newspapers could stomach. "The Stanfield Grazing
Bill," the San Francisco *Examiner* complained, "raids the public
lands. . . . America wants its public domain left free to the homesteader and the new farmer. It wants its national forests to remain
under the field control of the Forest Service, for conservation of
timber and water. The bill that turns over all these lands and watersheds, under perpetual contract, to the big stockraisers to use and
control and buy and sell as they see fit, is a noxious measure and
should be killed." It was.

If nothing else, the Stanfield bill brought the attention of Congress to the problems of the remaining public domain, and in an
effort to develop a leasing system for grazing purposes (not, however, by perpetual contracts) it passed in 1928 an act that set up an
experimental grazing district of 108,804 acres in the Mizpah-
Pumpkin Creek region of southeastern Montana. Under the act's
provisions, private stockmen agreed to lease public domain acreage jointly for a period of not more than ten years, a cooperative
venture reminiscent of the suggestions made by Powell in his *Arid
Regions* report of 1878. Before the Mizpah-Pumpkin Creek experiment could even begin to prove itself, however, Herbert Hoover
took office, bringing with him as Secretary of the Interior Ray
Lyman Wilbur, and these two Westerners, McKinley conservatives
by instinct, promptly formulated a plan to cede to the states in
which it lay all of the remaining public domain. As President

Hoover put it in 1929: "The federal government is incapable of the adequate administration of matters which require so large a measure of local understanding. We must seek every opportunity to retard the expansion of federal bureaucracy and to place our communities in control of their own destinies." It could not have been more succinctly expressed by John C. Calhoun, and Hoover pursued retardation by appointing a Public Lands Commission, the third in the nation's history. The Commission's report, issued in 1931, not only supported Hoover's plan but went on to conclude that "private ownership . . . should be the objective in the final use and disposition of the public domain." By 1931, however, Hoover's mind was occupied with other problems—the worst depression the country had ever faced—and "The Handout Magnificent," as Ward Shephard called it in *Harper's Monthly* never got beyond the stage of proclamation.

Depression or no, Congress finally faced up to the question of the remaining public domain in 1934, aided in this direction by gritty clouds of dust carried east from the overgrazed, overfarmed, and overexploited land of the Dust Bowl West, dust that was "the most tragic, the most impressive lobbyist," according to one observer, that Washington had ever seen. A solution, formulated by the Department of the Interior and the Department of Agriculture, was introduced, remarkably enough, by Representative Edward Taylor of Colorado, a backslid anticonservationist who nearly twenty years before had objected strenuously to governmental supervision of the public domain, declaring that the people of Colorado wanted to be "permanent citizens of the state, not federal tenants." By 1934 he had learned a good deal, as he later recalled: "I fought for the conservation of the public domain under Federal leadership because the citizens were unable to cope with the situation under existing trends and circumstances. The job was too big and interwoven for even the states to handle with satisfactory coordination. On the western slope of Colorado and in nearby states I saw waste, competition, overuse, and abuse of valuable range lands and watersheds eating into the very heart of western economy. Farms and ranches everywhere in the range country were suffering. The basic economy of entire communities was threatened."

Taylor's legislation, introduced as a "bill to stop injury to the public grazing lands by preventing overgrazing and soil deterioration, to provide for their orderly use, improvement, and development to stabilize the livestock industry dependent upon the public range, and for other purposes," met the expected assault in Congress from the representatives of the corporate stockmen, an assault as cynical as it was unsuccessful. Representative Ayers of Montana,

In these two photographs much of the history of the
American land is documented. Above, rich native grasses
spread to the mountain horizon; below, wind-driven dust
billows from land whose cover has been stripped away.

for example, introduced a substitute bill which provided that all lands in question be turned over to the individual states, and in testifying before the House Public Lands Committee he remarked that "In the last hearing you had here, a lot of men testified that overgrazing was the cause of erosion. Now, I hope there is not any member of this Committee that is going to be gullible enough to believe that." Representative Carter of Wyoming didn't believe it, either: "They want to prevent erosion to save the land for posterity. I want to say to you that if Secretary Wallace [of Agriculture] and Secretary Ickes [of Interior] were more interested in the erosions that are being made on the Constitution, they would do more for posterity."

The waving of shibboleths, states' rights, and outright lies was useless. The Taylor Grazing Act was passed and signed into law by President Franklin D. Roosevelt on June 28, 1934. Utilizing the Mizpah-Pumpkin Creek experiment as a partial model (in less than six years, the project had increased the stock-raising capacity of its land from 2,000 head to 5,000), Taylor's act provided for the formation of grazing districts on 80 million acres of the public domain (the acreage was raised to 142 million in 1935 and the limit was removed entirely the following year) and created the National Grazing Service to supervise it under the aegis of the Department of the Interior. These grazing lands were prohibited to entry under any of the existing settlement laws. A permit system similar to that operated by the Forest Service allowed stockmen to obtain leases on specified acreages for the grazing of specified numbers of animals for specified lengths of time (later called animal unit-months) at specified—if nominal—fees. Part of the grazing revenues would be applied to the counties in which the grazing districts existed, part to the Grazing Service, and part to the Reclamation Fund of the Department of the Interior. Any stockman could be denied renewal of his permit at the discretion of the director of the Grazing Service, with provision for appeal to the Secretary of the Interior. Officers of the various grazing districts would be aided by citizens' advisory boards (composed mostly of stockmen—unfortunately so, as it too often turned out). Finally, the act called for the Grazing Service to classify its land, with an eye toward not only grazing areas, but potential national forests, national parks, game reserves, mineral deposits, and water-power sites.

The revolution in land reform had been given its most significant legislation since the General Revision Act of 1891, and with its passage, an age had ended. "With the Taylor Grazing Act," Wallace

Stegner has written, "a historical process was complete: not only was the public domain virtually closed to settlement, but the remaining public land was assumed to be continuing Federal property, income-producing property to be managed according to principles of wise use for the benefit of the whole nation."

To some, however, more than an era had ended—the revolution itself had ended, a notion that might have amused John Wesley Powell, a man learned enough in the persistence of human shortsightedness to question the durability of any such grand finale. "The day on which the President signed the Taylor Act," presidential advisor Rexford Tugwell wrote in 1936, "laid in its grave a land policy which had long since been dead and which walked abroad only as a troublesome ghost within the living world." And as the last line in his splendid 1942 study of the public domain, *Our Landed Heritage*, Roy M. Robbins ended his assessment of the Taylor Grazing Act by declaring that "America had come of age."

Not quite.

VI
TWO-GUN DESMOND AND THE PARADOX FACTOR

ONE THEME THAT HAS RUN THROUGH this narrative with the consistency of a dirge has been what historian Bernard DeVoto described as the West's "historic willingness to hold itself cheap and its eagerness to sell out." Like most historic conditions, that willingness exhibited the strength and lasting power of tradition, an almost lunatic determination on the part of the West to act against its best interests whenever any clear choice was offered, to hamstring its present and mortgage its future. All in the name of progress, opportunity, individualism, and freedom—the first indefinable, the second closed to all but a few, the third nonexistent, and the fourth no more certain for Westerners than for anyone, anywhere.

Economically, that willingness had put the West in peonage to the East (and, to a lesser degree, to the financial centers of the Pacific Coast). It had allowed—indeed, invited—outside capital to enter the West for purposes of loot and rapine, to drain its minerals, strip its forests, exhaust its soils, clip its grasslands, control its cash flow, dictate its credit system, stifle its infrequent home-grown industries, dominate its politics, and convert its cities into company towns. The West whimpered fairly often, and shook an occasional fist, but for every nester who stood on the threshold of his dugout with a gun in his hand to keep from being run off his land by some ranch company, there were dozens willing to file false homestead claims for that same company for a reasonable fee. For every union miner ready to stake his job—and sometimes his life —in a strike against the Mine Owners Associations and the system

117

A cultivator of the earth and a legatee of the land and
its traditions: Francis Buck of Scott City, Kansas.

that kept him near the bottom line of poverty, there were scores who struggled to join that system by stealing from their sugar bowls to purchase mining stocks. For every newspaper editor who cried "Rape!" a hundred would drown him out with a pious chorus that advised the West that it was not rape, but love, and its child would be progress.

Environmentally, that willingness had brought the West the near ruination of the only asset it possessed—its land, had encouraged wreckage and waste, had given the land to be used as a pawn in the game of power played by the men DeVoto called "Two-Gun Desmonds," the romantic corporate cowboys, the sturdy corporate homesteaders, the grizzled corporate prospectors, the horny-handed corporate lumberjacks, together with the lawyers, merchants, and politicians who serviced their needs and parroted their philosophies. Like a man standing on the lawn in front of his burning house and handing cans of gasoline to the arsonist bent on destroying it, the West rallied around the Two-Gun Desmonds as they resisted the efforts of the federal government to save the West's land, the nation's land, as they fought the prosecution of land frauds, withdrawal of forest lands, establishment of grazing permits, protection of watersheds, creation of parks, regulation of timber cuts, attempts to limit the exploitation of water-power sites, irrigation sites, and mineral lands. And when the Desmonds finally had to accept, with however surly a reluctance, the presence of the government on the government's land, the West backed them to the hilt once again as they strove to subvert governmental regulations as they had once subverted land laws, holding one hand out, palm up, for federal subsidies and using the other to ward off federal supervision of federal land.

Hence, the paradox: the West crying "Freedom!" and bargaining away its life and heritage; the West crying "Individualism!" and tugging its forelock in the presence of corporate enterprise; the West denouncing "Paternalism!" and begging for federal handouts (without strings, please). That paradox had colored the entire history of the public domain, but never more grotesquely, more threateningly, more illogically than during the twenty years following the passage of the Taylor Grazing Act of 1934, a fact that drove Bernard DeVoto to one of his most eloquent dead-center observations: "The dissociation of intelligence could go no further but there it is—and there is the West yesterday, today, and forever. It is the western mind stripped to the basic split. The West as its own worst enemy. The West committing suicide."

As conceived, designed, and written into law, the Taylor Grazing Act was a needful and salutary measure, one calculated to carry over to the largest remaining part of the public domain those range-management practices developed over a period of thirty years by the U.S. Forest Service. Its long-range beneficiary would be the West itself, which might hope to see the continued protection of the land and watersheds without which it had no future. Its immediate beneficiaries, of course, were the stockmen, who received not only the same assurance of land and watershed protection, but were given the privilege of grazing on the public domain for fees so far below what it would have cost them on private land that they amounted to federal subsidies—five cents per cow per month on the range, or sixty cents a year, one cent per sheep per month, or twelve cents a year; if a man ran, say, 1,000 cows on 30,000 acres of public domain, it would cost him only $600 a year, whereas the use-rental of a similar block of private land might cost him five times that amount. The difference, though the stockman would have bristled at the notion, was a government handout.

All this being true, it should not be surprising to learn that the stockman, supported as usual by a good part of the West whose interests he would betray, almost immediately began a campaign to emasculate, and if possible eliminate, the whole program of range management. Emasculation came easiest, particularly during the administration of the first director of the Grazing Service, F.R. Carpenter, a Westerner with more than a passing sympathy for the stockman oppressed by bureaucracy (and after his retirement from government service, a lobbyist for stockraisers). "I am of the philosophy," he noted during a Denver grazing conference in January, 1935, "that the quicker land is put under private ownership, the better off the state to which it belongs will be. I am in favor of turning the government land over to the states and thence to the citizens as rapidly as possible." This remarkable statement—coming from a man whose appointed task was to oversee the wise use of land the government, his employer, had no intention of turning over to the states—was mitigated somewhat when he later said with visible regret that "The districts [grazing districts] are units of government, and thereby hangs a tale that may be with us for thousands of years." Shuddering at the prospect of a government unit lasting for thousands of years but cheered by the benevolent air of accommodation brought to his job by Carpenter, the stockmen proceeded to use the public domain pretty much as they always had used it—badly—formulating advantageous rules and regulations for the districts through the influence of advisory boards (composed of seven cattlemen, seven sheepmen, and one appointee of the Department of the Interior for each district), and systematically ignoring even those when they proved

OVERLEAF: A pastoral scene in the summer range country Salmon La Sac County, Washington. But what of the land?

inconvenient. The only difference now was that they had to pay for the privilege of misusing the land—a fact that rankled the sensibilities of the average corporate cowboy like a burr on the seat of his Ford pickup. Irritating.

Carpenter's successors proved to be less acquiescent. The Grazing Service, in fact, soon began to take its responsibilities seriously, not only cutting the allowable number of animals on land that had been visibly damaged, but advocating an increase in grazing fees that would be more in line with a fair price for the use of the public domain. Furious, the stockmen turned to Congress and found their champion in a new senator from Nevada, Patrick A. McCarran, who had taken his seat in 1934. McCarran was able, articulate, clever, and fearlessly dedicated to the interests of the stockmen's oligarchy that ruled his state like a sledge. As a freshman senator, he had bravely ignored the unspoken but traditional abjuration of his elders to shut up and listen by standing up and attempting to cripple the Taylor Grazing Act with an amendment that would have made it next to impossible for the director of the Grazing Service to revoke any lease permit.[4] "I do not propose to legislate the trail-blazers of the West out of existence," he said, "and I am not going to stand for it as long as I have vitality sufficient to resist it." The amendment did not survive, but McCarran had proved his virtue, and he quickly became the leader of a cabal of Western senators and representatives whose shields and bucklers bore the stamps of corporate trail-blazers. Much as the opponents of John Wesley Powell had done to control the obstreperous Major, they used the weapon of appropriations to put the Grazing Service in its place, systematically cutting the meat off its bones until it was left a skeleton agency. In 1941 they managed to get its headquarters moved from Washington, D.C., to Salt Lake City, where more direct communication (i.e., control) might be exercised by the users of the public domain. And in 1946, seizing the opportunity presented by the executive reorganization of the first Truman administration, they simply obliterated the agency by merging it with the old General Land Office to produce the Bureau of Land Management, which assumed the functions of both previous organizations—together with the carefully engineered millstone of Western domination.

McCarran and the boys had hardly started. Nor did they confine themselves to the remaining public domain. In 1946 Congressman (later Senator) Frank Barrett of Wyoming reintroduced his favorite bill, a measure that would abolish Jackson Hole National Monument and open its grandeur to exploitation (as on previous occasions, the bill failed), as well as one that provided for the sale of some 11 million acres of unorganized Taylor Act grazing land (also unsuccessful). McCarran himself took on the Forest Service by presenting his own perennial—a bill that would give grazing permittees what amounted to permanent property rights to their lease permits, including the right to buy and sell them or bequeath them to wives, sons, daughters, relatives, close friends, or charitable institutions (it too failed).

But the most ambitious and far-reaching bill introduced in that 1946 session of Congress—the most expansive such proposal, in fact, since the Hoover Commission report of 1929—was one presented by Senator Allan Robertson of Wyoming. First, it would have given to the thirteen Western states all unappropriated and unreserved lands and all homestead lands that had reverted to the national government through the years; it would be an outright gift, and it would include the rights to all oil, gas, and mineral reserves in such lands, with the proviso that oil, coal, and gas lands would have to be leased, not sold. There was more. The bill also would have established state commissions whose duty it would be to examine all national reservations within their boundaries —Taylor-Act lands, national forests, national parks, monuments, irrigation-district withdrawals, wildlife refuges, reclamation reserves, and power sites, in other words, all United States government land—to determine which could more effectively be administered (for which we may read sold, rented, or otherwise exploited) by the individual states.

It was a grand and wondrous scheme, the Robertson bill, one whose adoption would have eliminated the public domain. Unfortunately, it came to the attention of Bernard DeVoto, historian and writer by profession, a polemicist by instinct, and a Westerner by birth and heritage. Unlike the individuals and organizations who had for years been watching the Desmonds prepare for their raid and warning against it (among them lower-level officials in the Forest Service and the National Park Service, members of scattered and nearly powerless conservation organizations like the Izaak Walton League, the Wilderness Society, and the Sierra Club, and small stockmen and other Westerners who had learned to mistrust the corporate cowboys), DeVoto had a direct line to the public and a willingness to use it. For nearly twelve years he had occupied the "Easy Chair" column of *Harpers* magazine, one of the most prestigious and widely-read forums in the country. A self-proclaimed gadfly to the republic, DeVoto had already used the column to protest the suppression of war information by the government during World War II and the attack of blue-nosed censors on such books as Lillian Smith's *Strange Fruit*, and he would go on to use it to scold the F.B.I. for its tactics of snoop and to diagnose the *dementia praecox* of the McCarthy years. Like these issues, he immediately recognized in the question of the public domain considerations that raised it above the level of mere controversy; he could see—and express that perception with a vividness unmatched then or now—that the survival of the national inheritance of land was not only necessary for the survival of the West and hence of the country, but that it cut close to the heart of what America meant.

Armed with his historian's fund of knowledge, his arsenal of prose, and a body of information eagerly supplied by those whose voice he would become, DeVoto launched his attack in the January 1947 issue of *Harpers*—not in the "Easy Chair" this time, but in a full-scale article entitled "The West Against Itself." After briefly outlining the history of the West as the "plundered province" (as he had described it as early as 1934), he went on to clarify the peculiar psychology that enabled the West to simultaneously enjoy and resent its rape, to scream for the sheriff, as it were, while helping its attacker off with his pants. He then reminded his readers that "This is your land we are talking about," and proceeded to lay bare the provisions of the Robertson bill—not just its provisions, but its transparent intent:

> The public lands are first to be transferred to the states on the fully justified assumption that if there should be a state government not wholly compliant to the desires of stockgrowers, it could be pressured into compliance. The intention is to free them of all regulation except such as stockgrowers might impose upon themselves. Nothing in history suggests that the states are adequate to protect their own resources, or even want to, or suggests that cattlemen and sheepmen are capable of regulating themselves even for their own benefit, still less the public's. And the regulations immediately to be got rid of are those by which the government has been trying to prevent overgrazing of the public range. Cattlemen and sheepmen, I repeat, want to shovel most of the West into its rivers.
>
> From the states the public lands are to be transferred into private ownership. Present holders of permits are to be constituted a prior and privileged caste, to the exclusion of others except on such terms as they may dictate. They are to be permitted to buy the lands—the public lands, the West's lands, your lands—at a fraction of what they are worth. And the larger intention is to liquidate all the publicly held reserves of the West.

DeVoto's performance was a bugle call, a challenge, and a declaration of war. The public response astonished (and delighted) even him; he had for the first time on a national level articulated fears and resentments that had been bubbling in frustration under

There are not many photographs which do not require captions. This is one of them.

the lid the corporate interests of the West had placed over them, had tapped into an unsuspected source of common sense and righteous anger. Congress felt the pressure of that response quickly. The Robertson bill died aborning, proposed bills that had been drawn up to support its intention were stuffed into desk drawers, never to see the light of committee hearings, and McCarran, Robertson, and their colleagues hurried back home to explain to at least some of their constituents that they had not really planned to give away the resources of the West.

This is not to say that they had abandoned the cause—only that they would never again be tempted to embrace so large a concept as the Robertson bill. When the Forest Service announced proposed cuts in grazing permits in the spring of 1947, Congressman Frank Barrett took his House Subcommittee on Public Lands out into the West for hearings on the advisability of chopping back the Service's annual appropriation. DeVoto's spies and allies kept him informed of the committee's summer vacation and provided him with the record of its hearings, and in both an article and an "Easy Chair" column he cheerfully exposed the committee's bias and such asinine testimony as that given by the vice-chairman of the Joint Committee on Public Lands of the National Woolgrowers Association and the American National Livestock Association: "To me when you get a lot of federal bureaus operating and managing lands which are not the proper function of government provided in the Constitution, it is nothing more or less than a mild form of communism. And that malignant growth in the West is almost destroying the American form of government."[5]

The committee's purposes, as the stockmen's representative made abundantly clear in his little red-under-the-bed declaration, went beyond the mere chastisement of the Forest Service; after all, if the Desmonds could successfully maim the functional capacity of the nation's oldest conservation agency, how long would it be before they could have their way with the national parks, and how long after that would it be before they could do as they wished with the nearly 200 million acres of the remaining public domain? DeVoto did not hesitate to make precisely this point, and once again public reaction was substantial enough to block the enactment of any legislation that would have accomplished the committee's ends. And that remained the battleground for the next seven years: McCarran, Barrett, and their compatriots, backed up by various corporate associations (including the U.S. Chamber of Commerce, one of whose presidents in these years was himself a stockman) and the press they controlled or substantially influenced, would

In Bernard DeVoto's view, the confrontation between the land and the Two-Gun Desmonds was nothing less than a war. As in all wars, this one had its refugees, called migrants. Dorothea Lange caught some of them in 1936.

initiate forays against the public lands from various directions, some of them quite oblique; DeVoto and a growing cadre of conservationists, supported in Congress by such men as senators Richard Neuberger, Warren Magnuson, Eugene McCarthy, and Wayne Morse, would meet them at every turn, DeVoto turning the spotlight of publicity on them himself (not only in *Harpers*, but in *The Saturday Evening Post* and *Woman's Day*) and getting others to do the same, among them columnists Elmer Davis, Marquis Childs, and Joseph Alsop. As a result—as a *direct* result—the public domain survived. It survived the apathy of the business-oriented administration of President Dwight D. Eisenhower, whose attitudes toward the protection of the American land could have been inserted whole into the speeches of William McKinley. It even survived the demonstrable antagonism of Secretary of the Interior Douglas McKay, surely the least conservation-minded secretary in America's twentieth-century history (when conservationists rose up to oppose his enthusiastic endorsement of the Bureau of Reclamation's plans to build a dam in Echo Canyon, Utah, that would have flooded most of Dinosaur National Monument, McKay rummaged around in his mind for the precise word that would describe them with proper eloquence, and came up with "punks").

The public domain did not survive without injury. One such was inflicted when McKay was able to engineer the transfer of oil-rich tidelands—those offshore lands extending seaward three miles from the coast—from the Bureau of Land Management to the states of California, Texas, and Louisiana in 1953, leaving the United States in ownership of only the Outer Continental Shelf lands, a precedent that still worries those who would keep the public lands under federal ownership and control. Another was McKay's decision to turn over the power potential of the Snake River to the privately owned concern of the Idaho Power Company in that same year. Still, the national inheritance of land that had been defined and established with passage of the Taylor Grazing Act of 1934 had been preserved more or less intact by a dedicated minority of inheritors, a legacy to be passed on to a generation hopefully more attuned to the requirements of the future.

Bernard DeVoto, who died in December 1955, had been that minority's most vocal and most effective spokesman, producing a body of journalism that will stand, as Wallace Stegner has noted, as one of the most important chapters in the history of American conservation, a man whose ideas enriched the movement and whose language enlivened it. That service before his death earned him a lifetime membership in the Sierra Club and after his death a memorial grove of western red cedar in Clearwater National Forest. But his most suitable memorial, it can be said, is the continuing existence of the public domain itself and the growth of a philosophy that would not only protect and preserve it according to the rules and regulations of the past, but would develop a whole new body of law to keep it forever invulnerable to the blind assaults of Two-Gun Desmond and the paradox factor.

PART TWO:

THE INHERITORS

*"There are clarifications
as well as discouragements
in the study of history.
It demonstrates with
precision who the
adversaries are. Always are."*

—WALLACE STEGNER

VII
FOXES
AND GRAPES

IT WOULD BE PLEASANT TO REPORT that after more than a century of economic fiefdom, of watching its resources being gutted to no visible advantage to Western culture, society, or economic position—in fact, to their obvious detriment—the West had somehow found enlightenment. Pleasant, but not necessarily possible. True, the region's singularly roundheeled inclinations have been ameliorated somewhat by continuous exposure to the twentieth century, particularly by the remarkable blossoming of concern for the environment since 1960, a phenomenon that has seen conservation organizations such as the Sierra Club reach such a strength and breadth of influence that Congress has been known to listen to them on occasion with almost as much deference as it normally accords executives of General Motors. It is now a fact that in many parts of the West active conservation enclaves can be found, some of which are flourishing and most of which are not threatened by physical violence with any regularity. It is also possible to find many Western senators and congressmen who are willing to accept the fact—and state it for the record—that the American heritage of land is a trust that the federal government must administer for the benefit of future generations. It is even possible to find numerous newspaper editors in the West who will echo such sentiments from time to time. It is also heartening to find the Bureau of Land Management, born as the forceps child of the Grazing Service and the General Land Office in 1946 and catechized in its youth by the gospel according to Senator Patrick McCarran, reaching toward maturity, flexing its muscles and beginning to take its responsibilities seriously, as it was encouraged to do under the administrations of John F. Kennedy and Lyndon B. Johnson and less enthusiastically under those of Richard Nixon and Gerald Ford.

135

The Three Buttresses of Red Rock Canyon, Nevada—twenty miles and millions of years from Las Vegas.

Still, it is necessary to remember that Two-Gun Desmond is alive and well and preparing a memorandum to his congressional delegation, in spite of forty years of persecution by the "socialistic-minded collectivists" who have always been determined to destroy his freedom and sap the strength of America (the two being, of course, synonymous). He still has his spokesmen, even if their names have changed and their tactics become more subtle, and the influence they possess is still a force to be reckoned with in Congress. And Desmond still has a good part of the West backing him up, defeating its best interests, bargaining against its future, toying with its very survival. "SIERRA GO HOME!" proclaims the bumper sticker on the pickup truck driven by a hardware dealer in Anchorage, Alaska, who does not know or does not care that if "Sierra" does indeed go home the whole sad story of the Western experience will be repeated on America's last frontier, leaving him with a transient profit and his children with a can of ashes instead of a heritage.

The Nevada Prospectors and Miners Association, furious at the idea that the Forest Service and the Bureau of Land Management might impose fees for the privilege of using the public lands, is driven to petition Congress: "Resolved, we the following persons of the United States respectfully request our Senators and Congressmen reduce appropriations to the United States Forest Service by 80%, and reduce appropriations made to the Bureau of Land Management by 75%. The Forest Service (and Bureau of Land Management to a lesser degree) have entered upon programs and multiplied by the thousands, with no useful or constructive work to perform; but on the other hand have performed acts, and entered upon programs obnoxious and degrading to a free people. We . . . do not want their presence as a National Police Force to collect fees for a family man or his family to have a picnic, to be stopped and harassed for a $2.00 fee, or any other fee for eating a sandwich. Further, they have attempted to stop legitimate exploration, and entertainment with no seeming end except to legitimize their useless and unwanted presence. They are committing unbelievable acts of terror, such as public announcements that women and children and men who might pick up an Indian bead or arrow head laying upon the ground will be arrested. . . . We respectfully petition the Congress of the United States to reduce appropriations of the above agencies by the indicated percentages, as these funds are being used to establish a National Obnoxious Police Force." This same group—which claims to represent the "little guys" of mining—is appalled at the prospect that the General Mining Law of

1872 might be repealed and urges Westerners to "stand up for their rights," not knowing (or not caring) that it is precisely that law that has enabled an enterprise like the Carlin Mine of northern Nevada to tear up miles of desert in search of gold—gold that will not be used to enrich the citizens of Nevada but will be siphoned back into the coffers of the Newmont Mining Corporation of New York, the mine's owner and the land's user.

Richard Gerish of Reno, Nevada announces his candidacy for Congress in 1974 at a district office hearing of the Bureau of Land Management and proclaims that "I am here today to strongly oppose and object to the withdrawal of our public lands for wilderness areas. . . . If I am elected to Washington, D.C., I will request Congressional investigation into groups that hide behind environmental issues to help close down and withdraw our public lands. There is a growing demand for Congressional investigation into the Sierra Club and other radical groups like NORA [Nevada Outdoor Recreation Association], to see if there is collusion with these groups and BLM to stop the progress of our great nation. The gas shortage is because of these groups . . . caused by these un-Americans and environmental organizations that should be and will be investigated in the very near future. . . . I will also introduce legislation that would carry a severe penalty to stop progress in our country such as the environmentalists. . . ."

The "dissociation of intelligence," as Bernard DeVoto described it, remains in effect. Like the stone of Sisyphus, it is seemingly immortal, a constant drain on the energies of those engaged in the long, uphill struggle to give the public domain, that luckless pawn of history, the first intelligent management program it has ever known.

Recapitulation: the lands under discussion here, the lands that survived 150 years of corruption, speculation, giveaway, and wreckage, the lands that have been the target of another 40 years of attempted raids, the lands left over after all the various national reservations were made, are lands owned by the people of the United States—all of the people of the United States. These lands, the public domain, total approximately 471 million acres. Some 181 million acres of these lands are found in the lower forty-eight states and nearly all of them in the West (although there are 73,337 acres in various Midwestern and Eastern states, ranging from 43,882 acres in Minnesota to only 14 acres in Wisconsin). Nevada, with nearly 49 million acres, contains the largest single block of public lands in the West, but major portions of Utah, New Mexico, Wyoming, and Oregon are public domain, as are smaller but still substantial parts of California, Washington, Idaho, Arizona, Colorado, Montana, and the two Dakotas. The remaining 290 million acres lie in Alaska (including 143 million acres "alienated" under the terms of the Alaska Statehood Act and the Native Claims Settlement Act, although most of this land so far remains under the administration of the Bureau of Land Management).

For years, the public domain—especially outside Alaska—has suffered from a bad press; even those who have fought for its preservation have frequently assumed that it consisted of little more than godforsaken wastelands, bleak alkali flats, smelly sumps, and monotonous stretches of sand and sagebrush. In fact, it is quite as varied in all its characteristics as the West itself (not too surprising, since in many respects the public domain *is* the West), and is neither bleak nor forsaken by God. If a good deal of it is desert (and it might be useful to remember that the Son of God once walked in deserts), it also includes grasslands and prairie and tundra; mountain peaks as sheer and rock-ribbed as anything in Rocky Mountain National Park; swamps, lakes, streams, rivers, tarns, marshlands, hot springs, and geysers; forests of chaparral, oak, juniper, redwood, western red cedar, white pine, yellow pine, and bristlecone pine; flattopped mesas that float in the distance like mirages, spectacular canyons that look as if they had been sliced into the earth with a knife yesterday afternoon, and balancing rocks, toadstool rocks, caves, caverns, sandstone arches, and all the other geological formations carved by the hand of time; a zoological index of deer, antelopes, elk, caribou, moose, bears—black, brown, and grizzly—beaver, otters, coyotes, wolves, mountain lions, golden eagles and bald eagles, pelicans, peregrine falcons, and ospreys, and hundreds more, including such rare fish as the desert pupfish and the Utah cutthroat trout; and the marks of twenty thousand years of human history, from the delicate petroglyphs of prehistoric Indians to the axle-grease scrawls of wagon-train pioneers, from the cliff dwellings of the Anasazi and Moqui to the prospect holes of the new Jasons of the nineteenth century (for a more complete sampling of what the lands of the public domain have to offer in regard to all such values, see the "Wilderness Index" prepared by the Nevada Outdoor Recreation Association in the appendix to this book).

The public domain is a legacy of treasure, quite simply, and its caretaker is the Bureau of Land Management, an agency unique in more ways than one. Not only does this agency supervise the 453 million acres of public domain—more than all other federal agencies combined—it has some residual management responsibilities for millions of acres withdrawn for use by other departments, such as the Bureau of Reclamation, the Bureau of Sport Fisheries and Wildlife, and the Department of Defense. It administers more than 2 million acres of forest on Oregon & California Railroad lands (revested to the government in 1916) and on Coos Bay Wagon Road Company lands (reconveyed to the government in 1919), and another 2 million acres acquired by the government under the provisions of the Bankhead-Jones Farm Tenant Act of 1937 (which retired submarginal lands from agricultural production). It supervises all laws related to the disposal of public-domain lands (formerly the function of the General Land Office). In cooperation with the Geological Survey, the Bureau is responsible for the administration of the mineral laws on all public domain and acquired lands (including national forests and wildlife refuges), reserved mineral interests, and those on the Outer Continental Shelf. It keeps the basic public-land records and does boundary surveys for most federal lands. Altogether, the Bureau of Land Management has all or part of the responsibility for approximately 765 million acres of federal land.

The largest single portion of the Bureau's responsibility, as noted previously, lies in Alaska—and like the agency itself, the situation in Alaska is unique. First, the entire 365 million acres of Alaska were specifically excluded from all land laws when it was purchased from Russia in 1867, and the region did not enter the narrative of the public domain until 1884, when it was legally opened to prospecting (although a handful of its population of less than 500 non-natives had in fact been prospecting, staking claims, and mining for years, particularly in the region of Juneau). Not until 1890 was the Homestead Act extended to Alaska, where it proved quite as unworkable as it had on the Great Plains, and not until 1898, during the gold rush to the Klondike, were most of the rest of United States land laws made applicable to the region—not that it made much real difference, for it was not until World War II that Alaska had a population even large enough to qualify for statehood under the provisions of the Ordinance of 1787 (which required 50,000), and by the time of statehood in 1958 only 700,000 acres were privately owned. Second, when Alaska was made a state, it was also given the right to select no less than 103 million acres of land as its own over a period of 25 years—which, with an additional 45 million acres of tidelands, amounted to more federal land than that given to all the other Western states combined—and

OVERLEAF: One of the legacies of the Great Land, Alaska—the glacier first climbed by John Muir and named for him.

was further assigned the right to all mineral-leasing revenues that might come from its selections, together with 90 percent of the revenues from *federal* leasing (payments granted to no other state). Third, with passage of the Native Claims Settlement Act of 1971, Alaska's population of 75,000 Eskimos, Aleuts, and Athabascans were given the right to select 40 million acres, most if it in township parcels scattered over the immense land. Finally, that same act instructed the Secretary of the Interior to withdraw 45 million acres of public-interest lands for multiple-use mànagement by the Bureau of Land Management and another 80 million acres to be studied for possible use in the national park system, national forest system, wildlife system, and wild rivers system. And sitting in the middle of this whole complex situation, charged with administering most of the lands, making cadastral surveys so that state and Indian selections can be made, investigating lands to be put in national reserves, supervising mining and timber cutting on multiple-use lands, and balancing, adjudicating, and juggling claims and counterclaims is a beleaguered Bureau of Land Management.

Taken by itself, Alaska presents the Bureau with a huge responsibility, one it would be hard pressed to meet even if it had nothing else to do. As we have seen, the agency does have quite a bit else to do, but like the public domain itself the Bureau has from its beginning suffered from an overdose of neglect. It was founded by the minions of the Two-Gun Desmonds of the West to be nothing more than an interim caretaker of the land while they figured out some way of getting that land out of federal ownership, and the agency was for years deliberately kept short of money and manpower. Even now, when the Bureau has acquired the image of a steward of the land instead of a disinterested observer, it is understaffed, underfunded, and underpowered. It has 4,752 full- and part-time employees, and its budget for fiscal 1974-75 was set at $194,520,000. Just taking the 453 million acres for which it has full responsibility and ignoring its administrative duties on other federal lands, those figures indicate that the Bureau has one employee for every 96,000 acres and an operating budget of 42 cents per acre. By comparison, the Forest Service, with the responsibility for 187 million acres, has 9,415 full- and part-time employees and a budget for the current year of $544,260,310, which gives it one employee for about every 20,000 acres and an operating budget of $3.00 an acre. This is not to suggest that the Forest Service is overstaffed and overfunded; as it doubtless would be happy to point out, it, too, is probably short of what it needs. What this does suggest, however, is that the Bureau of Land Management is expected to operate in the real world on a staffing and funding system developed in some legislative wonderland.

If it is not given men and money enough to do its job, the Bureau is equally crippled by the fact that it has inherited intact the morass of confused and frequently conflicting regulations of its two parent agencies and that it possesses virtually no enforcement authority on the lands it administers. (If a Bureau field man spots a hundred minibikes wrecking the side of a mountain or catches someone walking off with a rock adorned with petroglyphs, his only recourse is to hop in his truck, drive to the nearest sheriff's office or police station, collar an officer of the law, and bring him back to the scene of the crime—by which time, of course, the dust of the minibikes would have settled and the rock be either gone or tossed to the ground). As Secretary of the Interior Rogers C.B. Morton has written, "Despite the enormous responsibilities of the BLM, the definition of its mission and the authority to accomplish it have never been comprehensively enunciated by Congress. Rather its mission and authority must be gleaned from some three thousand land laws which have accumulated over some 170 years and which are often at cross purposes."

Deprived of clear goals, adequate financing, needed staff, police power, and the ability to either formulate policy or suitably regulate what policy exists, it is not surprising to find that the Bureau has been driven to beg the public's cooperation through such advertising gimmicks as the Johnny Horizon clean-up campaign, to learn that it has been less than successful in its attempt to control off-road vehicle use on the public lands, that its regulation of mining, grazing, and timber practices has tended to be piecemeal and often ineffective, or that its disposal policies have too often been whimlike in their inconsistency—in short, that the Bureau has been powerless to give the public domain the care it needs.

What *would* be surprising would be to learn that nature would continue to tolerate this vacuum forever. It will not—but the manner and means by which the vacuum will be filled have yet to be determined.

The first stirring of change began a little over ten years ago, during the first administration of Lyndon B. Johnson and his Secretary of the Interior, Stewart Udall. It began with the passage, at the urging of the Department of the Interior, of three major pieces of legislation in 1964: the Public Land Law Review Commission Act, the Public Land Sale Act, and the Classification and Multiple Use Act.

The Public Land Law Review Commission Act created a body consisting of six members of the Senate, six members of the House, and six presidential appointees, together with an advisory council of twenty-five members. It was headed by Representative Wayne Aspinall of Colorado, chairman of the House Committee on Interior and Insular Affairs, and its stated function was to study "all existing statutes and regulations governing the retention, management, and disposition of public lands," to review "policies and practices of federal agencies administering these laws," to determine "present and future demands on public lands," and finally to issue a report at the end of 1969 (later extended to June 1970). The Public Land Sale Act (also scheduled to expire at the end of 1969) allowed the sale of comparatively small tracts of public land that were valuable chiefly for certain specified uses, such as sites for new towns, industrial sites, or other such major intensive uses. The Classification and Multiple Use Act directed the Bureau of Land Management to classify the public lands, determining which were suitable for disposal and which suitable for retention and management by the government under the principles of multiple use and sustained yield, thus carrying on the function first initiated by the Grazing Service but long since moribund. It, too, was scheduled to expire at the end of 1969, though both it and the Public Land Sale Act were later extended to December 23, 1970.

Chairman Aspinall, a devout Westerner in the tradition of Patrick McCarran (and nearly 70 years old in 1964), gathered his commission colleagues around him (most of them from the West, and many of them dedicated to the Aspinall persuasion), declared his intention ("I think we must find the means to provide for the transfer of much of this public land into non-Federal ownership and provide development"), and bundled off to the West for the first in a long series of hearings that would take place over the next several years. While neither so outrageously rigged nor so rambunctious as the hearings conducted by Congressman Frank Barrett in 1947, Aspinall's excursions were visibly biased and had their bad moments. For example, when George E. Hudson, Professor of Zoology at the University of Washington, attempted to read a two-page statement into the record during a hearing conducted at Spokane's Ridpath Hotel in September 1967, Aspinall cut him off in mid-sentence, declaring that the professor's comments on the pernicious effects of current range-management practices on wildlife were "irrelevant" and complaining that the commission was

There may be examples of more outlandish botanical archi-
tecture than the Joshua Tree, but one would be hard-pressed
to name them. It is common to the public-domain land of
the Mojave Desert of Southern California.

running out of time besides. He and another commission member then proceeded to harangue Dr. Hudson for several minutes ("Don't you eat food? Don't you wear shoes? Don't you live in a wooden house?"). When Dr. Hudson attempted to respond, Aspinall had him politely but pointedly removed from the room by the sergeant-at-arms. "The commission was very sympathetic to anyone who was asking for concessions for their own financial gain," Dr. Hudson later remarked, "and it prevailed throughout the entire hearing. It seemed very strange that a citizen who comes asking for handouts from the public trough should be treated with great kindness and time-consuming consideration—and one who is trying to protect the long-range interests of the nation in regard to the use of federal lands should be treated in quite a critical and unsympathetic way."[6]

While the commission criticized and sympathized according to its lights, the Bureau of Land Management was doggedly moving ahead with its assignment to classify the public lands. By 1969 it had classified some 180 million acres (31 million in Alaska) and of these had recommended nearly 150 million for retention for multiple-use and sustained yield purposes; in addition, six parcels had been classified as "primitive areas" to be considered for addition to the wilderness system (comprising 146,694 acres). Less than 5 million acres had been classified for disposal through sale or through the various land laws (an additional 20 to 25 million acres remained tied up in "checkerboard" sections carried over from the railroad grant days of the nineteenth century and were not classified). The response of the West, particularly from Nevada, was long, loud, and abundant. Writing in his *Golden Fleece in Nevada*, "lawyer, rancher, judge" (as he describes himself) Clel Georgetta typified the reaction: "Grab!—Grab!—Grab! . . . Nine million acres here, ten million acres there, and twenty million acres somewhere else will soon withdraw all the public domain from the possibility of ever becoming privately owned. Thus the Bureau of Land Management is spreading its permanent control over the face of the earth [!] in true bureaucratic, self-perpetuation style." The state's governor, Paul Laxalt, its two senators, Alan Bible and Howard Cannon, its congressman, Walter Baring, its Department of Conservation and Natural Resources, its Association of County Commissioners, its Committee on Federal Land Laws, mayors, councilmen, associations of stockmen and miners, and individuals spewed a stream of letters, resolutions, petitions, and telegrams to the Department of the Interior. And it worked. In the summer of 1969, classification of land in Nevada ceased, on the

No Stone of Sisyphus, but it might have been:
Balanced Rock in the Alabama Hills of California.

grounds, according to a letter from Nolan F. Keil, Nevada State Director of the Bureau of Land Management to Sumner L. Evans, director of the Nevada Outdoor Recreation Association, that "The Secretary's office [Walter Hickel at this time] is reluctant to permit classifications where such action is opposed by the Governor, the County Commissioners and state agencies." Nothing in the Act of 1964, it should be noted, provided for "reluctance" on the part of the Secretary of the Interior, and if his classification freeze in Nevada was not in fact illegal, it was a clear violation of the Act's spirit and intent. In any case, even though the freeze was lifted in the following spring, by the time the Act of 1964 expired at the end of 1970, some 8.6 million acres of public domain in Nevada remained unclassified.

If the Secretary of the Interior's classification freeze in Nevada had been a sore point with conservationists, the report of the Public Land Law Review Commission, released on June 30, 1970, was a disaster. It was entitled *One Third of a Nation's Land*, and to no one's real surprise it was only a little less accommodating than if it had been written by Two-Gun Desmond himself. "The most that can be said for the commission's recommendations on disposal," the Sierra Club's Executive Director Michael McCloskey wrote in August 1970, "is that 'wholesale' disposal of the public domain is not recommended, and that the disposal 'game' would not be played within the thicket of all the old disposal laws. The commission, however, would build a new and more efficient system to get rid of the public domain whenever a plausible taker can be found." Other conservationists agreed. "In a manner of speaking," one of them said, "PLLRC would like us to believe they are offering protection to the 'grapes,' while they actually withdraw it in deference to the foxes who want to eat them."

Consider the report's attitude toward the Bureau of Land Management's classification program: "We have found that the actions of the Bureau of Land Management under the Classification and Multiple Use Act of 1964 have paralleled to a considerable extent the liberal use of the withdrawal power of public land agencies. In less than four years [sic] under the 1964 Act, as of April 1, 1970, it classified 154.4 million acres of public land for retention, and either classified or 'identified' about 4.5 million acres for disposal. These classifications have a very substantial effect on land uses in the future. Despite the obvious need for careful planning, it is apparent that they were made in a hurried manner on the basis of inadequate information." As an antidote to this liberal overdose, the commission pointed out that it was within the power of Con-

The desert is a place patterned by the changing light; here, afternoon sharpens the edges of the Kelso Dunes.

gress to change these classifications any time it wished to, and recommended just that, with the additional proviso that all future withdrawals be made under a system whereby they would be "periodically reviewed and either rejustified or modified" (it is not difficult to figure out what was meant by "modified").

Consider the report's recommendation regarding the grazing lands of the public domain, the largest single part of the national inheritance: "Disposal of those lands which are principally valuable for grazing would reduce Federal Administrative costs. More important, it would place the management and use of forage resources in a free enterprise economy, and thus provide an incentive for the investment needed to make those lands fully productive. In private ownership economic efficiency would tend to cause the lands to move into hands of more efficient operators and thus lower the cost of livestock and improve the health of the industry." Let us make some definitions here. "Disposal" means selling the public domain in great blocks to those who could afford it at prices they would be willing to pay. "Free enterprise economy" means an economy free of the enterprise of any but the corporate cowboys. "Lands fully productive" means lands grazed with no protective restrictions. "Economic efficiency" means bookkeeping efficiency, an efficiency that does not place a dollar value on environmental degradation. And finally, "more efficient operators" means the large operators, the corporate operators, the operators who hire ranch managers to administer lands the owners quite often have never seen.[7]

Consider, finally, the report's approach to the needs of the mining industry—the *industry*, mind you, not the little old prospector with his burro and pick (or his Pace Arrow and metal detector). In the issue of *Metals Week* for June 29, 1970, the editor noted with considerable delight the mining provisions of the report: "The chapter of the report on mineral exploitation will be well received in mining circles. The philosophy of the Commission is clearly put forth in its first two statements of policy. 'Public land mineral policy should encourage exploration, development, and production of minerals on public lands,' and, 'mineral exploration and development should have a preference over some or all other uses on much of our public land. A decision to exclude mineral activity from any public land area should never be made casually or without adequate information concerning the mineral potential.'" The author of an article headlined "Mining's Public Land Prospects Soar" in the June 25, 1970 issue of *Iron Age* was even more entranced: "How close did the mining industry come to getting what

The public domain is a national treasure-house rich in
all the varieties of beauty, from the creosote bush of a
Southern California desert to the driftwood arranged on
the gravel bar of a high country river.

Tenacity: Above, a yucca plant etches beauty like lace in
a desert environment that does not encourage delicacy;
top, a bristlecone pine in the White Mountains of California, heavy with age and dignity.

it wanted in the Public Land Report? Generally, the report could not have been more favorable to mining interests if they had written it themselves." Desmond lives.

After the expenditure of more than $7 million, after more than five years of study and research, including thirty individual reports, after the combined thought and observations of 19 senators and representatives, 48 staff members, 25 Advisory Council members, 50 governors' representatives, 60 well-paid consultants, and more than 900 public witnesses, the Public Land Law Review Commission had produced a document that could have been scratched together in Aspinall's office by one of his administrative assistants without ever leaving Washington. Representative John D. Dingell, one of the few non-Western members of the Commission, had a few words to say about the reasons why: "There was hardly an all-out conservationist in the whole lot. On important environmental and conservation issues, I often felt that I was standing entirely on my own. . . . Outclassed, outnumbered, and outgunned, the national conservation and environmental problems inherent in the issues under study by the Commission were neatly smothered, ignored, or shunted below the dominant-use philosophy which characterized the approach of the Commission's membership."

The Commission's report mirrored the attitudes of President Richard M. Nixon (though there is no particular evidence to suggest that Nixon influenced the Commission directly; there would have been no need). As early as October 1968, while running for election, he had assured Nevada's Lieutenant Governor, Edward Fike, that his administration would initiate a completely new policy in regard to the public domain, declaring, among other things, that it did not "make sense" for the states—particularly Nevada—to own such small percentages of land within their borders. "Mr. Nixon agreed with me," Fike reported to the *Nevada State Journal*, "that Nevada must have more of its own land to put on the tax rolls and make available for residential and industrial expansion. He condemned the present administration's attitude of having the federal government hold so much land. He assured me there would be an entirely different policy. . . ." Even before the Commission had presented its report to him on the lawn of the White House in a suitably weighty ceremony, Nixon began implementing his—and the report's—philosophy. Early in 1970 he formed the Federal Property Review Board, with Presidential Counselor Bryce Harlow as its head, and issued Executive Order 11508, which directed all federal agencies except the Forest Service and National Park Service to list real property that was "not utilized, is under-utilized, or is not being put to its optimum use." When the various departments proved sluggish in making their lists, Nixon followed up on July 24 with an "administratively confidential" memorandum that somewhat testily demanded that the departments furnish the White House with an immediate report on that ". . . 10 percent of the property now held which is least utilized and has the lowest priority for retention. This report should be accompanied by a detailed plan for excessing [getting rid of] these properties." In addition, the president wanted a preliminary list by August 15, 1970, and a complete list by September 30 of all public property "ranked according to priority for retention."

Fortunately, the Nixon memorandum was leaked to columnist Jack Anderson, who exposed it on July 25. The reaction of conservationists, alarmed at the fact that the directive did not specifically exclude either the public domain or the nearly 28 million acres of wildlife sanctuaries, was immediate and eloquent. "I thought they were too busy plundering Alaska to pull off something like this," Representative John Dingell erupted. "Apparently, the President doesn't realize how hard we worked to save little bits of nature for wildlife sanctuaries. He doesn't realize that the nation's parks are terribly overcrowded on weekends. He doesn't realize that national parks like Yellowstone and Yosemite become outdoor ghettos in the summertime." What Nixon did not know, such organizations as the Wilderness Society, the Sierra Club, the Audubon Society, and the Wildlife Management Institute were willing to tell him, and did. A little over three weeks after Anderson broke the story, Secretary of the Interior Walter Hickel made public a statement that the wildlife refuges "are a priceless resource and certainly not considered 'surplus.' Our studies have shown that loss of habitat is the leading cause of loss of wildlife. Most of the endangered species on our list are endangered because they have been deprived by man of the natural habitat they need to breed and nourish their young. These wildlife refuge lands are now being used and we are continuing to acquire more." No mention was made of the public domain,[8] but the point of the conservationists had been made and had been heard. By February 1971, the Executive branch was making it perfectly clear that the "10% Sell-Off Scheme," as it had become known to many of the more militant conservationists, was of course applicable only to such lands as military installations, contractor-operated defense plants, federally operated airports, federal buildings and the land immediately surrounding federal buildings, and other such small and largely administrative properties. Later that

The domain of adventure: riverboats test the ripples, rocks, and rapids of the Rogue River through the wilderness defile of Grant's Pass, Oregon.

year Nixon himself noted grandly that "The public lands belong to
all Americans. They are part of the heritage and the birthright of
every citizen. It is important, therefore, that these lands be managed wisely, that their environmental values be carefully
safeguarded, and that we deal with these lands as trustees for the
future."[9]

Conservationists could take some comfort in the quick capitulation
of the Nixon administration in regard to the "excessing" of a good
part of the American land—some, but not much and not for long. In
April 1971, Representative Wayne Aspinall introduced The Public
Land Policy Act of 1971 (H.R. 7211), a proposal that embodied the
concepts outlined in the Public Land Law Review Commission's
One Third of a Nation's Land. Testifying before the House Committee on Interior and Insular Affairs, Michael McCloskey outlined the
crippling assumptions of Aspinall's bill: "These assumptions are:
(1) that federal lands should be managed more than they have been
with local interests in mind; (2) that more public lands which are
economically valuable should be put in private hands; (3) that multiple use should be re-oriented toward maximizing combinations of
uses, and that sustained yield should no longer mean maintaining
regular periodic output at a high level, but merely output at un-
specified levels at least cost to meet shifting markets; and (4) that
the administering agencies should be hamstrung in such a way that
curtails their freedom to make withdrawals to protect fragile envi-
ronments, and in a way that maximizes the influence of interests
which are intent upon obtaining increased emphasis upon commodity production." Specifically, Aspinall's bill provided that
only by special designation by a department or agency head could
any public land be selected "for a use inconsistent with State or
local zoning [a neat provision that was inspired by the fact that
planning agencies and legislatures in such states as Nevada,
Wyoming, and Idaho had already passed anti-wilderness
manifestoes]"; that "Each area or subarea having a dominant use
shall be managed under the principle of multiple use with as many
compatible uses being carried on as possible except that, in the
event of a conflict between uses [as, for example, between the dominant use of strip mining and the subordinate use of environmental significance], the dominant use shall, during the period of conflict only, prevail"; that the Secretary of the Interior be allowed to
make no withdrawals of more than 5,000 acres in extent (anything
larger would be the purlieu of Congress), and even those with-

*Denizens of the public land, its proper inhabitants:
Above, a mountain lion up a tree in Utah; below, a
red-tailed hawk contemplates its next meal
somewhere in Nevada.*

drawals be made in a mess of special rules and regulations, including a stipulation that none could be for more than ten years; and that the Secretary be ordered to review all land withdrawals made since January 1, 1956 and to furnish proof to Congress that any such lands should *not* be put up for disposal. Finally, the bill retained all the old land laws, including the General Mining Law of 1872.

Thus, a giant step backward for the public domain, one that matched in spirit, if not technique, the disposal practices of the nineteenth century. The bill remained in committee until June 14, 1972, when it was approved and sent to the floor of the House. To keep the bill's entrepreneurial dreams from becoming reality, a coalition of conservation groups, economists, and land-law and land-use specialists invested Congress with one of the most intensive campaigns in conservation history. It succeeded, and if the public domain did not receive its much-needed set of new rules in 1972, neither was it victimized by the ancient game of giveaway.

While opposing and defeating Aspinall's scheme, conservationists also put together a set of goals that any "organic act" concerning the public domain should attempt to meet. Briefly stated, these were:

- The repeal of the backlog of obsolete disposal laws and a confirmation of the national intent to retain all but a tiny fraction of the public domain in federal ownership, much along the lines of the Bureau of Land Management's classification program (154.4 million acres to be retained, 4.5 million to be disposed of).

- To make the Bureau of Land Management a permanent agency with broad, modernized management authority and a mandate to mark the boundaries of its holdings, name them, and regulate them with genuine police powers.

- The repeal of the General Mining Law of 1872 and the revision of the Mineral Leasing Law of 1920, replacing them with a mineral leasing system that could prevent mining whenever it conflicted with such other higher uses as environmental protection.

- The setting aside of those portions of the public domain most valuable as wilderness and wildlife areas—probably under less rigid classification standards than those imposed by the Wilderness Act of 1964, since many parts of the public domain have in fact been altered in some degree by man over the last century. Those "primitive areas" already classified by the Bureau of Land Management would be included in this program, and the 10 million additional acres that the Bureau has studied for possible wilderness classification would be protected for at least ten years or until their potential as wilderness had been determined.

A young burrowing owl. Like all his kind, he appears to be asking a question. Do we have the answer?

Born free and running free, pronghorn antelope
gallop to escape a low-flying plane, above. Below, a
herd of wild horses, running toward their
destruction, are rounded up by cowboys in 1944.

    With such goals in mind, conservationists steadily waged a
battle to dilute the toxic influence of *One Third of a Nation's Land*
and the residual effects of Aspinall's H.R. 7211, both of which
seeped into legislation with a debilitating regularity. (Aspinall's
own influence waned when he was defeated in his try for a thirteenth consecutive term during the 1972 elections; his place as
chairman of the House Committee on Interior and Insular Affairs
was taken by James Haley of Florida.) Gradually, through half a
dozen proposed bills between 1971 and 1974, conservation goals
came closer and closer to realization, culminating finally in
Senator Henry Jackson's bill, S. 424, the National Resource Lands
Management Act of 1973, which he introduced on January 18. During hearings before the Senate Subcommittee on Public Lands in
March, the bill was subjected to the standard assault of lobbyists
from the American Petroleum Institute, American National
Cattlemen's Association, National Woolgrowers Association, National Forest Products Association, National Coal Association,
American Mining Congress, and the American Farm Bureau Feder-
ation, each of which objected to the environmental "bias" of the
bill, and most of which strenuously advocated the incorporation of
the 5,000-acre withdrawal limitation of Aspinall's earlier proposal.
A phalanx of conservation representatives, on the other hand, endorsed the bill, with the qualification that it should include a section specifically repealing all or most of the land laws of the past
and one that would provide for wilderness review by the Bureau of
Land Management.

    This contest was won, for a change, by the conservationists.
After languishing in committee for more than a year during the
months of the Watergate miasma, Jackson's bill—complete with the
land-law and wilderness-review provisions—was reported favorably and sent to the floor of the Senate on May 2, 1974, where it was
passed by a vote of 90 to 1 in the late summer of 1974. The bill was
then sent to the House for referral to the House Subcommittee on
Public Lands. There, the Jackson bill came up against competitive
legislation, introduced by none other than the Subcommittee's
chairman, John Melcher of Montana. After being loaded down with
amendments tacked on by such legislators as Representative
Samuel Steiger of Arizona, Melcher's Public Land Policy and Management Act of 1974 (H.R. 16676) was approved by his Subcommittee on September 12 and sent to the House Committee on Interior
and Insular Affairs for consideration. Jackson's bill was not, nor
was an administration bill, H.R. 5441, somewhat less enthusiastically endorsed by conservationists.

As amended, Melcher's proposal, as Bernard DeVoto once described the Robertson Bill of 1947, was a sweetheart. First, it restricted, as did the Aspinall bill, the authority of the Secretary of the Interior to withdraw public lands from entry under the various land laws and the General Mining Law of 1872 in parcels larger than 5,000 acres; anything larger would have to be approved by subcommittees of both the House and the Senate. Second, it provided for the transfer of unlimited amounts of Bureau of Land Management recreation lands to state and local government agencies—and specifically turned over to the state of Nevada the 62,000-acre Red Rock Conservation Area near Las Vegas as an example. Third, it made a noble attempt to gut the effectiveness of the Endangered Species Act of 1973—which required federal land agencies to ensure that their actions did not jeopardize such species—by declaring that "endangered and threatened species shall be given equal but not greater consideration than other uses." Fourth—and in this respect it exceeded the grasp even of Wayne Aspinall's H.R. 7211—Melcher's bill allowed the forests, the *National Forests*, to be sold into private ownership at the whim of the Secretary of Agriculture, with first preference going to those timber, mining, and grazing interests already privileged in using them; it further required the "re-planning" of the Forest Service's 274 wilderness study areas and scores of natural areas established in the national forests. Fifth, it directed the Bureau of Land Management and the Forest Service to issue ten-year grazing permits (long a goal of stockmen) and stipulated that such permits could be renewed indefinitely, so long as a grazer had not directly violated regulations. Sixth, and finally, it allowed almost all the old land laws to remain in effect for another ten years. As a partial antidote to all this, the bill also allowed for wilderness review for public domain lands, established a multiple-use, sustained-yield mandate for the Bureau of Land Management, and established that agency as a viable, recognized, and permanent organization with some police powers, each of them concepts welcomed by conservationists.

Plus ça change, plus c'est la même chose. The cliché is applicable; it is, in fact, unavoidable. The names change, but apparently the powers and interests and motivations never do, nor does the vulnerability of the public domain. Most of the more outrageous provisions of H.R. 16676 were less the work of Melcher himself than of his Subcommittee staff, almost all of it inherited from the days of Wayne Aspinall and quite as committed as it always had been to the doctrines of Two-Gun Desmond. But once again these overachievers had gone too far; like Aspinall's 1972 bill, the

Melcher proposal encountered bitter opposition from conservationists, who managed to carve out those sections of the bill concerning the Forest Service and endangered species while the legislation was still in the House Committee on Interior and Insular Affairs. The bill never did get out of committee, in fact, but expired there as the 93rd Congress adjourned in December, 1974.

As Congress reconvened early in 1975, it was assumed that yet another public domain bill would be constructed and introduced into the House; that the Senate, having seen its own legislation come to a dead end in the House, would wait this time to see what would happen; that many Western representatives, particularly Arizona's Samuel Steiger, would attempt to cripple any reasonable legislation with amendments; and that conservationists would battle—again—for the passage of a bill that would give more consideration to the land than to those who would use it up. And while Congress pondered, struggled, debated, considered, and compromised, while it shuffled its papers, delivered its speeches, entertained both sides to every question, and articulated its frustration, the wreckage of that land continued.

A wildcat, frozen by a sudden flash of light and captured forever by the quick lens of a camera.

VIII
THE
PASTURES
OF HELL

THE YEAR IS 1886; the place, the High Plains. The narrator is John Clay, co-owner of the VVV Ranch on the Wind River of Montana: "By August it was hot, dry, dusty and grass closely cropped. Every day made it apparent that even with the best of winters cattle would have a hard time and 'through' cattle would only winter with a big percentage of loss. . . . Our neighbors kept piling cattle onto the bone dry range. The Continental Cattle Co. drove up 32,000 head of steers. The Worsham Cattle Co., with no former holdings turned loose 5,000 head or thereabouts. Major Smith, who had failed to sell 5,500 southern three-year-old steers, was forced to drive them to his range on Willow Creek near to Stoneville, now Alzada, Mont. The Dickey Cattle Co. . . . had brought up 6,000 mixed cattle from the Cheyenne and Arapahoe country and turned them over to their outfit whose headquarters were twenty or twenty-five miles below the above hamlet on the Little Missouri. Thousands of other cattle were spread over the western and northwestern country in the most reckless way, no thought for the morrow. . . ."

The "morrow" was winter, one of the longest and deadliest in the history of the West. And in the spring of 1887, the piles of dead cattle were stacked like rotting cordwood in the corners of barbed-wire fences, most erected to block the advance of the farming frontier. Their bloated, fly-ridden bodies clogged and poisoned the Yellowstone, Powder, Belle Fourche, and Platte rivers, cluttered gullies and gulches, littered the roadsides, and the stink of carrion hung in the air like swamp fog for months. "It was simply appalling," Clay wrote, "and the cowmen could not realize their position. From Southern Colorado to the Canadian line, from the

165

Grass—the essential cover for much of the public domain and too often the victim of the land's mismanagement.

100th Meridian almost to the Pacific slope it was a catastrophe which the cowmen of today who did not go through it can never understand. Three great streams of ill-luck, mismanagement, greed, met together. In other words, recklessness, want of foresight and the weather, which no man can control." And the land? Much of it was stripped of cover and lay naked to wind and rain. Much of it became desert within a span of ten years. Much of it took generations to recover. Some of it never did recover: in southeast Arizona there is a dry gulch 40 feet deep, 200 feet wide, and 60 miles long, where there was once a shallow stream valley crowded with grass and wild flowers; the date of the beginning of its ruin was the overgrazed summer of 1886.

The year is 1936; the place, Washington, D.C. The narrator is Henry A. Wallace, Secretary of Agriculture, who is making a report to Congress on the status and future of the Western range: "Further evidence of neglect is failure to regulate the use of range lands in such a way as to maintain the resource. This failure has been so general under all classes of ownership that in contrast examples of good management are decidedly conspicuous. The result is a serious and practically universal range and soil depletion, which already has gone far toward the creation of a permanent desert over enormous areas. . . . And three-fourths of the range area is still on the down grade. . . . The range problem as a whole has been allowed to drift for so long that its difficulties have been accentuated. It has become exceedingly broad and complex, beginning with the basic soil resource at the one extreme . . . to human welfare at the other. No single measure offers hope of more than a partial solution. One of the most important of the measures required is to place all range lands under management that will stop depletion and restore and thereafter maintain the resource in perpetuity, while at the same time permitting its use."

The year is 1974; the place, Boise, Idaho. The narrator is William R. Meiners, a thirty-year range conservationist and resource management specialist for the Forest Service, Soil Conservation Service, Bureau of Indian Affairs, and Bureau of Land Management; he is making a court deposition concerning range conditions in the 321,122-acre Challis Planning Unit of the Bureau of Land Management on the East Fork of the Salmon River: "The Public Lands of this Unit, and particularly those along the East Fork, are among the most abused lands I have seen in my entire professional career. Grazing pressure has reduced the lands along the river to almost a 'bare-ground' status. Under this pressure, the native perennial grasses which originally covered much of the land have been re-

Life in the cattle kingdom: Above, a herd gropes its way through a blinding Colorado snowstorm in 1900; below, a cow and her calf consider land stripped to nearly bare ground with the consent of their owners.

placed almost entirely by sagebrush with limited vegetation present beneath the sage plants. Severe and accelerated erosion is currently taking place together with streambank erosion and break down, producing sediment and debris which clogs and smothers the spawning beds and rearing areas of both resident and anadromous fisheries. . . . Grazing pressure has produced the same vegetative changes . . . in the rest of the Challis Unit, outside the immediate area of the East Fork. Here also erosion is evident, topsoil has been lost, meadows have been beaten into the ground, water is polluted, and exceedingly beautiful country has been diminished in its beauty and appeal."

Eighty-eight years have elapsed between Clay's experiences and Meiners' deposition, enough time for three generations of men with an accumulation of knowledge and experience and the expenditure of billions of government dollars to have achieved control over the three great streams of ill luck, mismanagement, and greed that have reduced so much of the West to a corrugated wasteland. Apparently, however, the time, the men, the knowledge, and the money have not been enough, and it is the public domain, the American land, that continues to suffer.

And make no mistake—it suffers. On approximately 160 million acres of land administered by fifty-two grazing districts, the Bureau of Land Management issues more than 15,500 permits each year for the grazing of 5.5 million head of cattle and sheep (and a few goats). Under present circumstances, the Bureau can do little to control the utilization of these millions of acres by these millions of animals. As noted in the previous chapter, the agency is undermanned and underbudgeted. On the local level, it has been frustrated by the influence of stockmen's advisory boards (established by the Taylor Grazing Act of 1934), which have been, after all, made up of men among whom the Bureau's field men and district officers must live.[10] In its own department, it is frustrated by decisions coming down from the upper levels in Washington, which are themselves unduly vulnerable to pressure from Congress, whose Western, stock-oriented members continue to exercise an influence beyond their numbers or the economic importance of the interests they represent. The result has been a repetition, in too many places and on too large a scale, of the patterns of waste.

In the Charles M. Russell National Wildlife Range of Montana (where grazing is administered by the Bureau of Land Management), erosion of the highly delicate bearpaw shale lands has caused

significant silt deposition in the Missouri River and encouraged
the infestation of sagebrush, rabbitbrush, and greasewood to re-
place the native grasses—all the work of overgrazing. In the Bear
Creek Watershed of eastern Oregon, overgrazing has caused extensive sheet erosion (loss of soil over a broad area) and gully erosion,
the destruction of all but a few perennial grasses, and the invasion
of sagebrush and cheatgrass. In the 200-square-mile Monticello
Grazing District of southern Utah, one of the major watersheds of
the Colorado River, the natural ground cover has been almost totally destroyed, leaving the desert land helpless in the face of flash
floods that have created erosion gullies so long and deep that they
can be, and often are, used as roads. In the Saylor Creek Unit of the
Boise Grazing District, which comprises 1,000 square miles, overgrazing has been a major contributor to pollution and sedimenta-
tion in Saylor Creek and the Snake River. In the San Simon Valley
of southeastern Arizona, so much of the land has been cropped to
bare ground that when it rains "the range melts away like sugar,"
according to a Bureau official.

The list could go on to depressing lengths, if it has not already,
and even then it would be only the sampling of a problem of huge
dimensions. Each year 500 million tons of topsoil is washed into
the rivers of the West. The Bureau of Land Management itself has
written that "There is very little of the western range where, because of the destruction of plant cover by improper management,
accelerated erosion has not destroyed a portion of the soil mantle,
and thus reduced the total productivity of the site" and in an internal memorandum has gone so far as to call grazing-induced erosion
this nation's "biggest source of resource deterioration and environmental degradation." The Bureau's own estimates in its
Budget Justifications report for 1973 put 84 percent of its land in
the "fair," "poor," and "bad" categories and only 16 percent in the
"good" or "excellent" categories. Much of the damage, as literature
from the Bureau's Washington headquarters has been known to
point out, occurred long before there was a Bureau of Land Management, or even a Grazing Service.

Much of the destruction, however, is not a legacy from the
environmental psychosis of the past. It is recent, it continues almost unabated, and it can be laid directly at the door of those
stockmen who are still dedicated to putting as many animals as
they can conceivably get away with on as much land as they can
find. They are not a majority, but they are a loud, insistent, and
politically influential minority, and they have grown accustomed
to getting their way with the agency designed to regulate them.

"Whenever we try to cut the number of cows," a Bureau official once complained, "a rancher will write to his Congressman, and pretty soon word comes down from headquarters: 'Let them graze.'"

Let them graze. The subject of precisely what it is they should graze has created another set of problems—not as immediately dramatic as those caused by overgrazing, but in the long run significantly damaging to the ecology of the West, at least the ecology that was meant to be. We talk quite a bit about the animals we have exterminated or brought to the verge of extinction. We talk a little less about the native grasslands we have destroyed. When the nearly uncontrolled grazing of the nineteenth and early twentieth centuries left so much of the land naked to the tools of erosion, it also left the land susceptible to the encroachment of such vigorous native cover as greasewood and creosote bush and the invasion of foreign plants and forbs, some of them palatable to wildlife and domestic animals, some of them not, but none of them indigenous to the land. Most of these invaders, like all migrating species, were durable and agressive, crowding out those native shrubs and grasses that struggled to recover from the assaults of cattlemen and sheepmen, stubbornly following in the paths of men, along his trails and roads and railway lines. In California alone (it leads the nation in this regard, as in so many other ecological matters), more than 290 individual types have invaded the hills and valleys, replacing much of the original ground cover of the Coast Range and Sierra Nevada foothills and totally replacing the ancient grasses of the California Prairie.

Some of these belligerent invaders have been foreign not only in the ecological sense but also in the national sense, including eleven Mediterranean and Australian strains. Some range botanists consider these to be of epidemic proportions in much of the West. The worst of the lot, however, is the toxic halogeton, a short forb of Ukrainian origin that is tough enough to grow where almost nothing else will and is capable of killing both cattle and sheep if an animal eats enough of it at a time (and while most wild creatures are too smart to eat the stuff, its presence does drive them from their traditional habitat). By 1940 this lethal bit of life had invaded the Great Basin, and by the end of World War II it had reached the epidemic stage. Stockmen, long accustomed to looking eastward in times of stress, set up a cry for help to Washington, demanding and getting "weed-control" legislation, and from that point on the Bureau's range-management program had less to do with regulating the way in which stockmen were allowed to use the land than regulating those plants that would be allowed to use it—namely, those which the stockmen wanted. This task was more easily accomplished during wet years, when the edible native vegetation was encouraged to try a comeback, but considerably less so in dry years when stronger foreign and unpalatable vegetation spread across the range like summer fire. There are, needless to say, more dry years than wet years in most of the West, and the Bureau was soon engaged in the practice of herbicide on a wide scale, utilizing such exotic products of American chemical technology as 2, 4-D; 2, 4, 5-T; and tordon (all three were found to cause fetal abnormalities in mammals, presumably including man, and were placed on a restricted list by Interior Secretary Walter Hickel in 1971).

Another technique developed in these years was the chaining and reseeding process called range conversion, in which great stretches of native and undesirable vegetation are removed from the land by dragging an immense barbed chain (some of them a hundred feet long and weighing several tons) between two bulldozers, then reseeding the exposed earth, usually with an exotic called crested wheatgrass. Millions of acres have thus been converted—or, in the lexicon of the stockman, improved. Unfortunately, the highly palatable replacement is dependent upon regular spring rains for healthy growth, a phenomenon that no part of the arid and semiarid West can count on, and when the crested wheatgrass has disappeared, the Russian thistle, the cheatgrass, and the greasewood are never far behind.

By accident and by design, then, the exertions of man have profoundly changed not only the contours of the Western range, spilling much of the land into its rivers, but also the very mantle that had covered it for millennia. The alteration continues with deadly inexorability—so much so that serious consideration is now being given to the creation of a Grasslands National Park on the Great Plains, so that it will be possible for the future to see, somewhere, that great "sea of grass" that awed those who, in the words of James Bryce, "first burst into this silent, splendid nature."

If we are bringing ruination to the physical nature of the Western range, we are doing little better for the wildlife that is has supported for at least as long as man has been on this continent. The grazing animals—the various deer, elk, pronghorn antelope, bighorn sheep—must compete for every blade of grass even on healthy land, and on land that has been seriously overgrazed the struggle to survive, particularly in the winter, is a bitter, continuing, and too

OVERLEAF: "A cow is the God-damndest dumbest critter that ever walked the face of the earth," a cowboy once said.

often a losing fight. In many areas the populations of these animals have diminished dangerously. Bighorn sheep, for example, which are extremely wary of men and are not particularly fond of cows, either, have been driven from their historic winter range by domestic animals, making them undernourished in the months when heat-supplying food is most necessary and leaving them prey to parasites, pneumonia, and stress; in some regions bighorn sheep herds have been reduced by as much as two-thirds in recent years. Hundreds of miles of fences on the public domain also have interfered with the migratory patterns of forage wildlife. The destruction of native vegetation has eliminated booming grounds and nesting areas of sage grouse. Sediment and debris from erosion have muddied the streams and rivers, smothering the spawning beds and rearing areas of both resident and anadromous fisheries. Herbicides have sickened whole populations.

All this might be called incidental depredation, neither planned nor wanted, just irresponsible. But there is another kind of killing going on in the lands of the public domain, a kind so careless, so wanton, so needless—and yet so desired—that it suggests an almost pathological irreverence for life—all life, including that of the killers. We are not talking here about hunting, which is called a sport. We are talking about killing, which is excused as a necessity. It is done both privately and by the government—state and federal—and it is done for the most part at the insistence, and quite often with the participation, of the Western stockman. It has already eliminated the mountain lion from most of the West and reduced the population of wolves to a mere 500, most of which remain in Minnesota, some of which survive in a sanctuary at Isle Royal, Michigan. The killing is now—as it always has been—aimed especially at the coyote, but it sometimes seems that every small creature that moves upon the earth or flies through the air may be in the killer's sights. The creatures are called varmints; except for the eagle, they are unprotected by law, and in the view of too much of the West, their function in life is to die.

The excuse is that such predators as coyotes, bobcats, golden and bald eagles, and crows—yes, crows— are positively decimating, in almost the literal sense of the word, the cattle and sheep herds of the Western range. These animals always have been, the stockmen say, and they always will be unless they are eliminated. The stockmen have tried, most diligently. They have shot thousands of coyotes from airplanes, in cooperative roundups, by jack-lighting at night, by summer dog runs, and by winter snowmobile hunts, in which the hunters communicate with one another by citizens-band radio. When individul effort is not enough, those who operate on private land call in state trappers and those who graze the public domain call in the trappers employed by the United States Bureau of Sport Fisheries and Wildlife, an estimable agency in charge of administering the nation's wild things. Until 1972 the use of such poisons as cyanide, strychnine, and sodium monofluoroacetate, otherwise known as 1080, made such administration most efficient: in 1971, at a cost of $8 million, the poison program of the United States government killed 89,653 coyotes, 24,273 foxes, 20,780 bobcats, and 842 bears, calf and lamb killers all, according to feverish stockmen. Unfortunately, a poison does not know what it is killing, and in that same year the United States government also eliminated such additional "predators of livestock" as 19,052 skunks, 10,078 raccoons, 7,615 opossums, 6,941 badgers, 6,685 porcupines, and 1,170 beaver. Since the eagle has been protected by federal law for more than twelve years, government trappers could do little about its assault on Western livestock. Still, many hundreds of eagles over the years were killed accidentally by picking up poisoned bait meant for other animals, and thousands more were shot—quite often from airplanes—by ranchers, in spite of the law.

It is all worth it, the stockmen say, even the risk of a $500 fine and a jail term, even the expenditure of millions of dollars of taxpayers' money over and above the subsidy they receive in permit payments to graze on the public domain. The killing must continue, they say. We cannot survive without it, they say. There is no doubt that they are convinced. When President Nixon banned the use of most predator poisons on federal land with his Executive Order 11643 in February 1972, they set up a howl of protest that is still reverberating. Yet there is a kind of dementia loose here, a distortion of intelligence, a willingness to accept and perpetuate transparent myths and statements that come close to being downright lies. In 1973 Nevada sheepmen claimed that they had lost 32,000 sheep to predators the previous year, the equivalent of more than *one-seventh* the total population of sheep in Nevada, a figure that is impossible to believe. One sheepman maintained that he had sold his herd of 2,500 because he was losing from ten to thirteen sheep a night to coyotes, which suggests that packs of coyotes (who do not travel in packs) would have been able to eat his entire herd in something over eight months of steady gorging. Another sheepman, this one in Wyoming, states with a straight face that the average eagle will kill two lambs a day—one for breakfast, then "he will nail another one for supper. Luckily for us sheepmen,

the typical eagle usually skips lunch." Of the many studies under-
taken over the years, none has ever indicated that eagles have developed a predation pattern for lambs, and only one, conducted
from 1967 to 1969 in Texas, was actually able to find evidence of
any predation; the slaughter included eleven lambs in one of the
years, four in another. Still another sheepman says unequivocally
that the common crow, which is a scavenger, not a predator, will
land on a newborn lamb, peck it to death, peck a hole in its skull,
peck out the brains, eat them, then peck a hole in its belly and eat
the innards. That would be one hungry crow.

And what of the coyote, that deadly stalker of calves and lambs
and even full-grown sheep? "In fifty years and two generations,"
Oregon cattle rancher Dayton Hyde testified before the Senate Subcommittee on Environment in 1973, "we have not lost one single
animal to predators. A small band of stray sheep wintering un-
tended on my ranch lost not one single animal, although coyotes
were ever-present. . . . Year after year, the same old pairs of coyotes
maintained their same territories and we knew many as individuals. Their pelts were good and knowing where every mouse run
and brown squirrel hollow was in their range, they made a good
living and bothered nothing."

Colorado rancher Tom Lasater, whose Beefmaster cattle are
famous the world over, has not been quite so lucky as Hyde. In
nearly twenty-five years of running his 25,000-acre ranch on the
plains between Limon and Colorado Springs, he has lost a total of
two calves to coyotes, both in 1971 after a drought had reduced the
animals' natural prey. He did not call for trappers, neither did he
load his shotgun and hire an airplane to track his coyotes down and
kill them. Lasater does not kill anything. He does not kill coyotes,
prairie dogs, bobcats, raccoons, foxes, or porcupines. He does not
even kill weeds. He has posted his land as a wildlife area and he
operates it as such. And, to the befuddlement of his neighbors, who
have been killing things for generations, Lasater's ranch produces
fat, unpreyed-upon cattle, his range is healthy, and he flourishes.
And so does the wildlife that surrounds him.

Both Hyde and Lasater have learned to operate on the principle
that it is better in both the short run and the long run to use the land
well and to respect the creatures who share it with them. It is not
"ecology" so much as it is plain, visible, demonstrable common
sense. But they and those others who share their feelings are a
decided minority among the stockmen of the West, most of whom
will not give up the killing that has long since acquired the patina
of tradition and the compulsions of ritual and will not even aban-

*This is what overgrazing means. This is what erosion
looks like—here, in Utah, and in too much of the West.*

don the delusions by which they convince themselves that it is necessary to their survival. They have always killed things, and so long as they have their way they will go on killing things until that time when, as Jack Olsen has written in *Slaughter the Beasts, Poison the Earth*, "the last weak and sickened coyote will drag himself to his feet and lift his voice to the skies and there will be no answer."

The trapping continues, with live bait and "passion" bait now, for the most part, and so does the shooting. There is even the strong possiblity that cyanide poisoning will return to the public lands. In May 1974, the Environmental Protection Agency—the Environmental *Protection* Agency—launched an experimental program in twenty-one Montana counties to test the efficiency of a relatively new poisoning device. Called a coyote-getter, this gadget employs a spring-loading mechanism that fires a spray of sodium cyanide into the animal's mouth on contact. It is said to be wonderfully effective.

Ever since passage of the National Evironmental Policy Act of 1969, it has been suggested that one method whereby continued misuse of the grazing lands of the pubic domain could be halted would be to have the Bureau of Land Management file unit-by-unit environmental impact statements for each Grazing District before the renewal of any grazing permits. Instead, the Bureau chose to interpret the requirements of the Act more loosely, putting together a single environmental impact statement for all of the 160 million acres of grazing lands. Neither its Preliminary Draft Environmental Impact Statement, issued early in 1974, nor its Draft Environmental Impact Statement, issued in June, 1974, was received with much enthusiasm by conservationists, who objected that no single such statement could possibly give the lands the detailed analysis required of any normal report. One conservation organization, the Natural Resources Defense Council, objected so strongly, in fact, that in March 1974, (and with the support of the Nevada Outdoor Recreation Association, among others) it brought suit against Rogers C.B. Morton, Secretary of the Interior, and Curtis J. Berklund, Director of the Bureau of Land Management, declaring that the Bureau had not satisfied the requirements of NEPA, was not in the process of satisfying them, and would not satisfy them until it was willing to issue individual unit statements.[11]

The purely legal arguments in the case, quite as complex and obfuscatory as such arguments usually are, need not concern us

Two kinds of killing: The first, above, is deliberate, and those who practice it exhibit a kind of pride. The second is inadvertent, if inevitable, as mismanagement destroys the habitat of such animals as the ruffed grouse.

here. What is important is that the government's legal response to the allegations of the suit leads one to believe, if he did not believe before, that only when Congress passes legislation that recreates the Bureau of Land Management as a viable working agency with precisely defined duties and powers will it ever be free of the influence of Two-Gun Desmond and his politicians. Aside from the occasional petulance of that response (at one point, it stated that "Plaintiffs' suit seems to be based upon a suspicion that they will not like the statement when it comes out and that they know better than the Department of the Interior how an environmental impact statement should be prepared"), it presented two arguments that seem suggestive. The first was that for the Bureau of Land Management to withhold temporarily grazing permits in any given area while preparing the required statements would be to inflict undue hardship on those accustomed to using the lands of the public domain—a stand which seems to imply that the environmental interests of the land should be subordinated to the economic interests of those who have demonstrated themselves capable of destroying it. The second argument was even more curious. Making the assumption that the real purpose of the suit was to eliminate grazing on the public lands altogether (which the quickest reading of the suit would verify as ridiculous), the government's argument maintained that NEPA requires an impact statement only when an action is likely to have significant adverse effect on the environment in question, and since the grazing of domestic animals already was taking place on the lands, there could therefore be no adverse impact and the Bureau was consequently not required to file a statement (then, one wonders, why did it?). It bolstered this argument with the most curious statement of all: "If grazing ceases [which no one but the respondee has so far suggested], the lands accustomed to grazing would receive a sudden environmental shock that would cause a chain reaction throughout the ecosystem. The indigenous fauna would be forced to change their accustomed migration patterns. Some of them would die out while others would increase in number. A similar sudden ecological upset would occur among the flora now present in these areas." Grazing is good for the land; not grazing is bad for the land. The Doublespeak involved in the statement becomes all the more obvious when it is placed against the Bureau of Land Management's very own Preliminary Draft Environmental Impact Statement, which had another version of what would happen if grazing ceased: "Animal control practices for protection of livestock would not be required. As a result all wildlife species would have an improved opportunity for survival. . . . Some threatened species of wildlife will be more assured of survival. Wildlife populations would increase when food cover and water is reserved for wildlife. . . . The mortality of wildlife by starvation will be reduced when competition with domestic livestock is removed. The source of domestic stock diseases and parasites transmittable to wildlife would be removed. Bighorn sheep and deer populations may respond favorably and extend their ranges to historic habitats.''

The pastures of Hell versus the pastures of Heaven. The schizoid nature of the two visions indicates something more than a traditional breakdown of communication between lower and upper levels of a bureaucracy. It suggests that the officials at the top are listening, right enough—but not to their own people.

Addendum: There is a magazine advertisement going the rounds these days, sponsored by the American Sheep Industry. It is headlined "NO MORE LAMB. NO MORE WOOL. IT COULD HAPPEN." The text is a quote from an "American sheepman," and it goes on at some length to describe the sorry state of the sheep industry and all that it means to America, and concludes "You could get along without lamb and wool. It's not a life and death matter for you as it is for our sheep. But with so many shortages these days, it just makes sense to preserve all the natural food and fiber we can. At the same time, we'd be holding onto something precious, a good way of life for our children and our children's children. No more lamb? No more wool? Let's not let it happen."

Just below the text there is a photograph. It shows a lone man, his faithful shepherd collie gazing up at him, his loyal horse at his side. The man is staring moodily across an empty landscape to a deserted sheepherder's cabin. The land on which this lonely corporate cowboy is standing, the land that spreads out beyond him for thousands of acres, is stripped as clean and smooth as a pool table. It is overgrazed.

IX

CHITTY, CHITTY, VA-ROOM, VA-ROOM

SILENCE IS PERHAPS THE MOST IMPRESSIVE thing the desert has to offer. There are sounds, of course—the distant chattering of birds, the skittering rustle of small animals, the muted rattling of creosote bush and greasewood touched by the wind. Yet these sounds only serve to emphasize the vastness of the desert's essential silence—a stillness that clarifies the enormity of the space that surrounds you. It is incredibly beautiful, this delicate collaboration between space and silence; you do not shout, for fear that the sound will shatter the balance and go sweeping across the bleak and bony country like fire in a tinder-dry forest.

Suddenly you hear a low rumbling. You look to the mountains, but there are no clouds to indicate a distant storm. The birds have stopped singing. A scrubby little desert rabbit bustles out from behind a bush and heads off across the desert floor. He is followed by several others. A coyote follows them, but he has no visible interest in rabbits at the moment. The rumble by now has become a dull, steady thundering.

And then, on the crest of the horizon, you see them.

Motorcyclists, thousands of them, too many to count, too many to estimate, too many to believe. They are strung across the landscape like some grotesque reenactment of the Oklahoma land rush, bounding over rocks, grinding through sand washes, flattening creosote bush, leaping arroyos, challenging the cracks and lumps and dangers of the land in a frenzied game of hare and hounds. Behind them, a dust cloud a mile wide and two hundred feet high billows into the flat blue sky. As they reach and pass you, the sound is a scream and bellow that pummels your eardrums and shakes the ground beneath your feet. Helmeted and goggled, their faces lost in grime, the riders race remorselessly on until they are dimmed by the dust and the distance, and their sound declines

183

An abandoned car waits for time in the Mojave Desert.

OVERLEAF: Motorcyclists on their way to "Fun City" via the land.

once again to a rumble, a whisper, and finally, after a long time, to nothing.

The air reeks of gasoline, oil, burned rubber, and the acrid smell of exhaust fumes. You walk across the wide path the motor-cycles have taken and note what they have left behind: shrubs and needlegrass and cacti mutilated, the seedbeds of all the delicate desert flowers disturbed perhaps beyond recovery, the earth itself maimed and rutted by tire tracks that cross and criss-cross in a demented maze. In an hour or so the wind will clean the air of the dust and the stench, but nothing can be done to repair the earth, not now, not for years, or to muffle the pounding roar that continues to echo in your mind. . . .

The preceding vignette is not a fantasy. It is a report. Every year, the 16 million acres of public domain that lie in the Mojave and Colorado deserts—Southern California's "backyard"—are witness to similar scenes on a year-round basis. In recent years the 200-mile Barstow to Las Vegas Thanksgiving Day race has become tremen-dously popular. In 1974, for example, it included no less than 4,000 motorcyclists, who roared off to "Fun City" along a two-mile-wide front, in spite of a legal protest by the Environmental Defense Fund and the Sierra Club. Such phenomena are called events, and they are but the most dramatic manifestation of the increasingly critical conflict between machines and the land of the public domain, po-tentially the most destructive threat to the semiwild environment of this land since the invention of the internal-combustion engine. In too many areas it is not a conflict, it is nearly uncontrolled assault, an infestation of an absolute welter of motorized gadgets: motorcycles, trail bikes, Land Rovers, Jeeps, and other four-wheel-drive vehicles, dune buggies, snowmobiles, minibikes, and those contraptions that the Volkswagen people call The Thing. It is now possible for all but the poverty-stricken to own *some* kind of machine that will enable them to zip across more landscape in a day than they would be able to negotiate in two weeks of hiking. And they do.

The conflict is not a new one. The determination to drive a motor vehicle anywhere he damn pleases is one of the oldest and least endearing characteristics of twentieth-century man. More than sixty years ago, automobilists managed to pressure their way into none other than Yosemite Park, in spite of a warning from James Bryce: "If Adam had known what harm the serpent was going to work, he would have tried to prevent him from finding lodgement in Eden; and if you were to realize what the result of the automobile will be in that wonderful, that incomparable valley, you will keep it out." William E. Colby, the otherwise militant secretary of the still-new Sierra Club, disagreed: "We hope they will be able to come in when the time comes, because we think the automobile adds a great zest to travel and we are primarily interested in the increase of travel to these parks." Bryce's result, of course, was a national disgrace, and if Colby were alive today he would doubtless be striking his breast with *mea culpas*.

This conflict is not new, and not yet resolved or even close to being resolved, although the Bureau of Land Management has been giving it a dedicated try for more than ten years. When it became apparent to the Bureau in the early 1960s that recreational-vehicle use on the public domain was going to become a significant factor, the agency launched an extensive study to make recommendations to the Department of the Interior that would give it the power to regulate such use. In the meantime the Bureau did what it could to stay on top of the situation through education and by seeking the voluntary cooperation of various vehicle groups. Unguided by any firm federal law (who could have foreseen such a thing as a dune buggy?), it had little choice. "This is a new kind of use of the public domain lands," the Bureau reported in a 1968 brochure. "A few years ago it was a relatively unheard of sport; today, it constitutes a major, and growing, recreational demand."

"Demand" was the correct word. Well organized into suitable enclaves (desert-riding cycle clubs, the National Association of 4-Wheel Drive Clubs, the American Trail Bike Association, the American Motor Scooter Association, the American Motorcycle Association, etc., etc., etc.), relatively affluent, and extremely active wherever and whenever their sport was questioned, none could have been more cognizant of their rights than the vehicle enthusiasts. For years they stubbornly fought even the idea of any kind of restrictions. In an article written for the Spring 1969 issue of *Cry California*, I quoted motorcycle writer Bob Greene, whose attitudes seemed to me typical of those of the time: "Confining motorcycles to specific areas is not the answer. Everybody wants to tell the other guy what to do. Do you want to be told where you can drive your car?" (In that same issue, I answered his question: "For Mr. Greene's information, I might point out that I *am* told where I can drive my car—I can't drive it the wrong way on a one-way street, I can't drive it on railroad tracks, sidewalks, library steps, or in hotel lobbies; in short, I am forbidden to drive my car anywhere that a car has no business going, where it would unnecessarily

WAWONA

endanger life, limb, and property or disturb the public tranquility. Can as much be said for motorcycles and the public land?") Even today, when most groups have adjusted to the idea that they are going to have to give in to federal regulation—particularly the four-wheel-drive associations—resistance to regulation can sometimes be downright arrogant. When the Bureau of Land Management attempted to persuade the El Cajon Valley Motorcycle Club not to hold a December 1972 race in an area rich in archeological value, the club ignored the plea, protesting its right to do so on the grounds that "the public lands should be free."

The fact is that while not every off-road motorcyle rider is a potential candidate for the Hell's Angels nor every driver of a four-wheel-drive vehicle a beer-can-dropping troglodyte, strong legislation to govern their operations has been needed desperately for years, for their impact on the land and other users of the land is tremendous. Consider motorcycles and trail bikes, for instance. As many as seventy-five of the "hare and hounds" races described at the beginning of this chapter take place in the deserts of Southern California every year, involving thousands of participants and their machines. At least another 150,000 cyclists visit the desert non-competitively each year. The total effect of all this activity is difficult to measure, but some idea can be gained from the Bureau of Land Management's own conviction that any piece of land that is used repeatedly by motorcyclists can be written off for any other recreational uses. "Motorcycle wheels rip out vegetation and tear up the soil," a Bureau pamphlet reported in 1969. "Clouds of dust cover untouched vegetation and the topsoil blows away. The tire tracks become eroded gullies. . . . " In a more detailed report the Bureau outlined the results of one weekend of cross-country racing: "Measurements on a one-acre plot were taken at a parking area and starting point for a cross-country trail where 900 vehicles (including motorcycles, automobiles, trucks, campers, and trailers) were gathered. The plot showed that 58 percent of the woody vegetation was destroyed or irreparably damaged. The slow rate of growth of one particular species, creosote bush . . . which covers approximately 78 percent of the desert, precludes it from becoming a dominant wind or water control device for at least ten years." When this kind of damage is inflicted on the hillsides of a forest, as it often is, it can mutilate watersheds by greatly accelerating the natural course of erosion. One powerful little trail bike, grinding its way straight up a hill softened by rain, will gouge out a groove that can become a stream during the next rain, a rapid little creek the next, and a miniature torrent the next, until the entire hill is crip-

Automobiles on their way to the "incomparable valley"
of Yosemite through the Wawona Big Tree, 1924.

pled, much of the ground cover gone, tree roots exposed, and the ecology altered.

The effects of motorcycles and trail bikes on wildlife is more difficult to measure, but in 1968 the Wildlife Management Branch of the California Department of Fish and Game was moved to make some educated assumptions: "Indiscriminate motorcycle riding and other off-highway vehicles would have adverse effects on wildlife, especially on bighorn sheep, nesting birds, and on young broods of wildlife. . . . " In 1972 Wilbur W. Mayhew, professor of zoology at the University of California at Riverside, was more succinct: "In the last ten years I have seen with my own eyes more than a 50-percent drop in wildlife [in the California desert]."

Private livestock, much of which is grazed on public lands, is also susceptible to this kind of harassment; ranchers with grazing permits have complained of stampeded cattle and sheep often enough for the Bureau to have a sizable file on the subject. But it is when motorcycles and trailbikes encounter people on hiking trails and in camping grounds that the conflict between uses of the public domain becomes real even to those who may not be impresed with damage to land and wildlife. The encounter can never be anything but painful, and often is dangerous, as Bob Denning of the *Arizona Republic* indicated while describing the progress of one motorcycling pilgrim through his campsite: "On he charged. Right through camp. Dodging the cars. Just missing the cook fire. Pebbles across the dinner table. Zig-zagging through the bedrolls. Then, down through the arroyo and across the far ridge. . . . Those back-firing two wheelers spook game, ruin naps, destroy plants, encourage erosion, infuriate hikers, unsettle horses, madden dogs, shatter picnics, bomb birdwatchers, sadden stump-sitters, and for all I know, probably adversely affect the weather."

The situation is not improved by the addition of smaller two-wheelers called "minibikes." They are not speedy, but they are powerful and are small enough to be tossed into the trunk of a normal-sized automobile and carried right to the edge of whatever chunk of the public domain their owners might care to invade. They are enormously popular (at least 100,000 are in use in California alone) and cheap enough to be within the reach of small boys who deliver newspapers for a living. There is some indication, in fact, that a whole new generation of cross-country vehicle enthusiasts is being bred. A recent issue of *Boy's Life*, the official magazine of the Boy Scouts of America, contains no less than seven advertisements for minibikes, ranging in price from a $49.95 build-it-yourself model to a $189.95 item, complete with ski acces-

Killers of time, killers of land: Above, mindless tourists
have scrawled over ten-thousand-year-old petroglyphs, and
sharpshooters have used the figures as bull's-eyes. Below,
a souped-up Beetle helps convert the land to a dirt track.

sory. The advertisements emphasize the minibike's ability to travel over any kind of terrain: "The all-season trail bike that goes anywhere—in the boondocks or on the street . . . in mud, sand, brush, even snow." As the kids mature, it can be expected that they will graduate to bigger and better machines.

To one degree or another, the dune buggies, snowmobiles, and four-wheel-drive vehicles exhibit the same impact upon the land as the motorcycle and its mutants. Even viewed in the most favorable light, all are uncontestably destructive to wildlife, irritating and even dangerous to those human beings who get in the way, and most are capable of effecting major, long-range damage to the land—annihilating vegetation, ripping up watershed areas, creating new areas of erosion, and generally lacerating what it took the natural order of things eons to evolve.

Beyond this, these vehicles are frequently utilized as tools in a different kind of destruction. "Pot-hunters" use them to gain access to archeological sites so that they can gather up pot shards and arrowheads; they call themselves collectors. Others, and we can call them vandals, use them to get close enough to petroglyph sites to use the drawings for target-shooting, or improve upon these ancient art forms—many of them as much as 17,000 years old —with spray paint and chipped-out initials. Others simply chisel or blast particularly splendid samples out of the rock and carry them home, possibly to make lamps or coffee tables of them. Still others (motorcyclists, mainly), whose motivations would be the proper study of psychopathologists, have discovered the immense primitive intaglios etched into the rock-like earth of many places in the Mojave and Colorado deserts; they have mounted their motorcycles, broken down fences, and deliberately and repeatedly scarred the intaglios until many have been all but obliterated. The theft and vandalism (both federal offenses under the Antiquities Act of 1906) have become so widespread and so impossible to prevent that the Bureau of Land Management has instituted a policy of silence in regard to new discoveries, hoping to protect them from those who would steal from time.

The machines are on the land, and they are not going to leave. We can deplore the fact, if we wish, but the fact remains that recreational-vehicle use in this country has become a powerful and incontrovertible force, one with political and economic influence and one determined to have its share of the public domain that belongs to all of us. We need to accept it—perhaps as reluctantly as

Secretary of Agriculture Earl Butz accepted the existence of the environmental movement in a speech before the National Wool Growers Association in January 1973. "The conservation movement," he said, "is here to stay, and we're going to have to learn to live with it." We need to accept the off-road vehicle in order to control it and engage the cooperation of those who use it to ensure the continued preservation of the public domain.[12] The beginning of control was established in February 1972, when President Nixon issued Executive Order 11644, which ordered federal public land agencies to "establish policies and provide for procedures that will ensure that the use of off-road vehicles on public lands will be controlled and directed so as to protect the resources of those lands, to promote the safety of all users of those lands, and to minimize conflicts among the various users of those lands."

A little less than two years later, the Bureau of Land Management issued an environmental impact statement "pertaining to use of off-road vehicles on the public lands," and four months later issued regulations for the management of the use of off-road vehicles. Among those regulations were provisions that required licenses for all off-road vehicles, established a permit system for any meet, race, or other large event, authorized the Bureau to collect fees and levy fines, and allowed it to close any area to off-road vehicle use. Conservationists were willing to cheer this as a good start. They would have been happier if the Bureau had set up a system by which lands were closed to off-road vehicles until investigations and hearings established that they should be opened, rather than leaving the lands open to such use until investigations and hearings established that they should be closed. They would have been even happier if the Bureau had been given genuine police powers to enforce its rules.[13] And they would have been happier still if the Bureau's total field force in 16 million acres of the Mojave and Colorado River region, the largest single area where the largest single use of off-road vehicles takes place, had been more than the eight men now in service.

X
THE
ANATOMY
OF CRUNCH

WE KNEW—we *had* to know— that it could not go on forever. But we were like the alcoholic who knows that at some point he will have to sleep, and then wake to the horrors of the day after, but who will not think of that, perhaps cannot think of that, can think only of finishing the glass in front of him, buying another, finishing that, and buying another, and another, until his metabolism finally fails him. And, like the cynical bartender who busily hustles the customer before him, insensitive to the destruction he is fueling, concerned only with the next six bits he can ring into the till, we were encouraged—indeed, urged—by an entire industry to indulge our blind consumption of energy, to buy just one more self-cleaning electric oven, one more 285-horsepower automobile, one more air-conditioning system, one more stereo system, one more electric heater, one more electric tie rack; to keep our houses at 80 degrees in the winter, 65 degrees in the summer; to travel as often and as far and as fast as we could get away with. And we did. We bought it all.

"Sooner or later in life," Robert Louis Stevenson wrote, "we all sit down to a banquet of consequences." Ours was presented to us in the form of what some of us called an "energy crisis" or an "energy crunch." Others pointed out that it was a hangover, the inevitable result of a thirty-year energy binge. Even for those who believe that the gasoline and heating-fuel crisis of the winter of 1973-74 was at least in part a manufactured inconvenience, a neat gimmick calculated to justify a price increase (which certainly occurred) by the time-tested system of artificial shortage, the experience at least stands as a kind of dress rehearsal. And we are likely to have several more, each becoming progressively more legitimate,

195

Energy as mess: A broom used to clean up oil from the beaches, docks, and boats of Santa Barbara, 1969.

until the final one is so genuine that even the oil companies will be damaged by it. Since 1965 the consumption of oil in the United States has increased each year at the exponential rate of 4.5 percent over the consumption of each previous year—like compound interest in a savings account, only in this case we are withdrawing, not depositing. So long as we maintain that yearly consumption rate, there is nothing we can do that will prevent the irreversible crisis that will come, probably within twenty years.

Our "oil deficit"—the difference between domestic extraction and domestic consumption—has increased at the rate of some 300 million barrels a year since 1971, and at the end of 1973 had reached nearly 2 billion barrels. Our own resources cannot hope to match such a deficit. Even the oil reserves of the Arctic Slope, that bone of contention between environmentalists and the oil industry for so many years, probably include no more than four years' worth of oil at our present rate of consumption (and less than that, of course, since it has been learned that the industry plans to sell much of that oil to Japan). Increased importation from the Arab states, as Robert Entwhistle has written, "may require that we sell our economic soul—and even that solution would be temporary, since like our oil, our soul is probably finite."

Clearly, if there is a solution it must be in energy conservation, not energy development. Yet instead of placing a restrictive tax on gas-eating chariots or alloting a couple of hundred million dollars for the development of a 100 mile-per-gallon automobile, the government subsidizes the jet-airplane industry, the least energy-efficient system in the world. Instead of throwing enough money and energy behind the creation of urban mass-transit systems and the revitalization of the nation's railroads, the government finances a $50-billion interstate freeway system, whose principal beneficiary is the trucking industry, a transportation system with an energy inefficiency second only to that of the jet airplane. Instead of making any firm commitment to energy conservation, in other words, the government seems convinced that faith and free (that is, government-subsidized) enterprise will somehow postpone the day of reckoning, that we should produce more, not use less.

And caught in the path of this singularly stubborn "go-ahead" philosophy, vulnerable as always to the machinations of those who would use it up, is the American land, the public domian.

Item one: millions of acres of the American public domain are under water—a fact that has kept discussion of them out of most of this narrative, for obvious reasons. But they are still part of the public lands, a basic resource owned by all Americans. They are the lands of the Outer Continental Shelf, a government-owned piece of the ocean that extends from the three-mile limit to the twelve-mile limit off the coasts of the United States (the area from the edge of the coasts to the three-mile limit was granted to the individual states in the Tidelands Act of 1953). Until our technology made it possible to sink drills scores and sometimes hundreds of feet through the water to the ocean floor, the government ownership of these lands was little more than a curious fact. When that technology developed, however, when it became possible to build drilling and pumping platforms out in the middle of the ocean, to lay pipelines on the floor of that ocean between the platforms and the land, to build onshore refining facilities to process the oil produced from such platforms, ownership became a responsibility that demanded legislation to govern its administration, establish a leasing system for its oil wells, and safeguard its environmental quality. That legislation was provided with the Outer Continental Shelf Act of 1953, which placed these lands under the jurisdiction of the Bureau of Land Management.

The development of oil "fields" proceeded apace, and by 1970 there were 7,000 oil wells operated by 53 individual companies off the coasts of California, Texas, Louisiana, Mississippi, Alabama, and the panhandle of Florida. Inevitably, there were accidents. Just part of the price of progress, the oil companies said—regrettable, but nothing we could not learn to live with. Others wondered about that, particularly when they examined the record of oil-spill problems in the Gulf of Mexico, where hundreds of minor and major spills took place every year. They wondered about it in the face of the fact that between 1960 and 1970 nine accidents involving drilling or producing operations resulted in the spillage of 102,500 barrels of oil; that two pipeline accidents in 1967 spilled another 167,000 barrels into the sea; that wastewater discharge contributed the aggregate of another 9 barrels of oil a day into the ocean. They wondered about the price of progress when Union Oil's No. 9 well in the Santa Barbara Channel blew its cap in January 1969 and spewed millions of gallons of oil into the sea off Santa Barbara, killing vast numbers of birds and fish and other forms of marine wildlife, turning the lovely southern California surf into a turbid gray sludge, staining yachts and littering the sand with thick pools of oil; when Chevron Oil's "Platform Charlie" exploded into flame in February 1970 and sent a huge fan of oil into the Gulf of Mexico; when Shell Oil's own platform exploded in December 1970, bubbling its

Energy as perpetual motion: Oil pumps rise and fall in an endless saraband, sucking the fuel that feeds growth from public-land oil leases near Hays, Kansas.

oil into the sea, clogging oyster beds, invading wildlife-rich estuaries in the Mississippi Delta, poisoning the coastal waters. They wondered at the oil companies' assurances that the price of progress was inevitable when they saw Chevron Oil being indicted on 900 counts of violations of the safety regulations of the Outer Continental Shelf Act, pleading "nolo contendre" to 500 counts, and being fined a million dollars.

They began to wonder, finally, whether the price of progress might not have something to do with our very survival. Studies made on a small oil spill off West Falmouth, Massachusetts in November 1969 indicated that the pollution expanded steadily after the initial spill, until it covered most of the eight square miles of Buzzard's Bay. In the immediate vicinity of the spill, the oil killed 95 percent of the adult organisms of the environment within a matter of days and did not lose its toxicity as it spread out; eight months after the spill, contamination was still so bad that commercial shellfishing would be banned for at least another two years. Further, the action of the rough sea "emulsified" the oil and spread it through the water column, much of it settling on the bottom, where it killed larvae organisms necessary to the recovery of the area.

Aside from such direct pollution from oil spills, the long-range effect of oil development on such estuarine regions as the Mississippi Delta-areas where the very stuff of life is nourished and enriched— can be lethal. Here, both development and pollution have destroyed marshes and wetlands to the tune of 200 square miles—16.5 square miles a year, a rate that, if it continues, will sooner or later convert the Delta's carefully-balanced land-water ecosystem to a monstrous complex of man-made canals and deep-water lakes.

We have proved ourselves incapable of controlling or even keeping up with the rate of oil pollution that exists off our coasts under the present level of production. To increase that production significantly would increase the incidence of pollution in mathematical proportion and forever eliminate any hope we might have of getting the situation in hand. To increase production under such circumstances, obviously, would be to invite disaster. It would be an act of irresponsibility, an act so blind to the realities facing us that only someone deprived of simple common sense would advocate such a thing. Early in 1974, President Richard Nixon announced the goal of leasing an additional 10 million acres *a year*, and on November 13, 1974, the Department of the Interior announced that it was proposing to lease an additional 17 million acres a year—as much as has been leased altogether since 1953—including 2.6 million acres off the coast of northern and southern California, nearly 6 million acres in the Gulf of Mexico, and 3.5 million acres off the Middle Atlantic coast. President Gerald Ford enunciated the thinking behind this dramatic announcement: "We must adopt rigorous conservation measures. But it is clear that regardless of what conservation steps we take and what eventual long-range energy policy we adopt, in the near term we must increase our domestic production of oil and gas."

Item two: the idea of tapping into the earth's own "steamrooms"— her geothermal deposits—for the power to generate electricity is not a new one. In California the Pacific Gas & Electric Company has been operating a geothermal generating plant near Geyserville in northern California for two generations. Only recently, however, has anyone been inspired to develop this resource on a major scale, and like the decision to open up the lands of the Outer Continental Shelf to oil leases, the inspiration was manufactured by the current infatuation with the idea of producing more and more energy. Once again the national lands are involved, for virtually every one of the major feasible sites for potential geothermal development exists somewhere in the public domain.

The mechanics of establishing a leasing system for a "national geothermal energy program" were outlined in the Geothermal Steam Act of 1970, and after its passage the Bureau of Land Management put together leasing and operating regulations, wrote up an environmental impact statement as required by the NEPA, and beginning in January 1974 began accepting applications for leases. Private and public utilities companies were not bashful in applying: during the month of January the Bureau received 2,456 applications covering 5.2 million acres scattered through California, Nevada, Oregon, Washington, New Mexico, Idaho, Utah, Colorado, Montana, Arizona, and Wyoming. Nevada alone had received 780 applications concerning 1.7 million acres of land by the end of the following month. The newest twist in the energy game had found a large number of hopeful participants.

Too many, and too fast, according to most conservationists. If the decision to double in one year the leased acreage of the Outer Continental Shelf had been one that flew in the face of observed reality, the decision to throw open millions of acres of the land-locked public domain to geothermal development was one made in the environmental dark. In its own environmental impact statement, the Bureau of Land Management had admitted, by implication if nothing else, that it simply did not know what the impact of geothermal development would be on the ecology of any given region. The statement is packed with splendid generalities, but no specifics to speak of—and many of those generalities appear ominous enough to be justification for the immediate halting of the program until more detailed and accurate studies can be made, possibly through some pilot program.

For example, the statement points out that blowouts—the sudden loss of control of a steam source—"pose a distinct environmental hazard," but how much of one it does not say. It says that the release of particularly noxious gases into the atmosphere might be an adverse effect, but it does not define "noxious." It admits that the noise involved in released steam would be a disturbance to wildlife, that the release of toxic or highly saline geothermal waters into nearby freshwater sources would damage fisheries and waterfowl nesting and feeding areas, that heated effluents would be likely to "alter aquatic habitat and life," that poisons and corrosive fluids could contaminate surface waters, and that the ground-water level in any geothermal area might be changed for all time. The document states that "the potential for a major quake cannot be ruled out" because of changes in reservoir pressure, subsidence, and land compaction that will follow the release of steam on any massive scale, surely the most ominous generality of them all. In short, the Bureau's environmental impact statement, the document that is supposed to let us know to what extent and for how long any development is likely to damage the environment, is a collection of uncertainties whose very existence places the geothermal energy program in a bad light.

In spite of the uncertainties and the potentially deadly effect of geothermal development, the government has cried "Full steam ahead!" in another almost thoughtless capitulation to the demands of energy growth.

Item three: Offshore oil development poses known environmental hazards; geothermal development poses unknown but possibly significant environmental hazards. Our third entry in the energy crisis versus the American land poses both, and in quantity, but its effect, already being felt, goes further: it could transform not only much of the land itself, but alter beyond all recognition the life styles that have inhabited it for generations, could, in fact, change a predominantly rural, agricultural land into one more anthill of urban progress, together with all that goes with it. We are talking about the leasing of chunks of the public domain in the high plains and Rocky Mountain regions for the purpose of strip-mining for coal and oil shale—leasing it at prices that do not come close to a fair value, leasing it to a handful of major corporations who are not likely to care one thin damn for the quality of the life they will destroy, leasing it for the enrichment of a few and the poverty of the land and the people. And it will be all of us who will lose.

It is estimated that some 57 percent, or 850 billion tons, of coal in the United States is found west of the Mississippi River, and most of this is in the region of the high plains, including parts of North Dakota, South Dakota, Montana, and Wyoming; other huge deposits are also found in Colorado, Utah, and New Mexico. Oil-shale deposits are more confined, most of them existing in south central and southwestern Wyoming, west central Colorado, and east central Utah, but they are still estimated to contain 600 billion barrels of potentially recoverable oil. Although some are found on private lands (to which the government owns the mineral rights) and some on Indian lands, most of these coal and oil-shale treasures are found on the lands of the public domain.

Spurred on by the demand for more energy sources, particularly by the Project Independence efforts of the Federal Energy Office, the leasing of these lands has been accelerated by the government over the past several years, and there has been no shortage of takers. A total of 680,854 acres of coal lands in the West have been taken up in 463 individual leases under the provisions of the Mineral Leasing Act of 1920. Seventy percent of this leased land is held by but fifteen corporations, among them Continental Oil, Shell Oil, Gulf Oil, Arco, and the Peabody Coal Company (which leads the list with 49 leases and 174,352 acres). Unfortunately for the hopes of Project Independence, however, only 52 leases are being worked to produce coal; the remainder are being held for a rise in the price of coal. Nor can it be said that the people who own the lands—that is, the citizens of the United States—have received fair value for them. The average winning bid, on those rare occasions when there was more than one bidder, for these leases was only $2.87 an acre, and the royalty payments to the government for the coal that has actually been worked has amounted to 12.5 cents a ton.

An even more marked example of consolidation and ridiculous prices was found in the oil-shale leases. It was not until the end of 1973 that the Department of the Interior launched its Proto-type Oil Shale Leasing Program, which called for the leasing of six 5,120-acre (or eight-square-mile) tracts, two each in Colorado,

Energy as death: Above, an oil-soaked bird at Santa
Barbara, 1969, the victim of human carelessness. Below,
the land gutted by an earth-eating machine, victim of
what can only be called human greed.

Utah, and Wyoming, and not until January 8, 1974 that the first sealed bids were opened in the Denver office of the Bureau of Land Management.[14] In the March 1974 issue of the Sierra Club *Bulletin*, David Sumner related the momentous occasion: "Everyone laughed in nervous relief when the first bid—a token, sardonic one dollar, plus 49 percent of the profits—was announced. When the second sealed envelope was opened, the mood changed sharply. BLM prognosticators had figured a maximum bonus bid of about $50 million; onlookers gasped and started buzzing when a consortium of Marathon Oil, American Petrofina, and Phelps-Dodge came in with a flat $80 million. The third bid stopped the place cold. The ante of Standard Oil of Indiana and Gulf Oil was announced at $210,305,600, and as one observer noted, 'I thought they'd have to bring in 20 stretchers.'" Apparently, the Bureau's people had not been paying attention to their own figures. They had estimated the recoverable oil shale in the first tract to be somewhere in the vicinity of four or five *billion* barrels; Standard Oil and Gulf Oil were not making some incredible gift to the United States—they were getting the rights to all this oil for something like five cents a barrel. So far, only one other tract has been leased, this one to a consortium of Arco, Shell Oil, and Ashland Oil for a bid of $117,700,000. The Department of the Interior, however, has already selected an additional seventeen tract sites for possible future leasing and has announced plans for the next century that would include somewhere between thirty-five and sixty individual plants turning out oil at the rate of three to five million barrels a day.

Almost all of the coal of the public domain and most of the oil shale will be strip-mined, a prospect that makes conservationists cringe. Strip-mining, as any afternoon's drive around in the wreckage of Appalachia will suggest, may possibly be the single most *ugly* form of land exploitation that exists—and that includes a lot of forms. Thousands of square miles of land would simply be gutted by the enormous machines the industry has developed through the years; one of these beasts, a 7,000-ton, 200-foot-tall monster called The Gem of Egypt for some peculiar reason, is already chewing its way across much of Ohio, and machines like it will doubtless be gobbling away at the West in a few years. Nor is there much realistic hope that the land so mined can ever be reclaimed. While provisions in existing law require reclamation, while current legislation in Congress will require a higher percentage of money be paid in by coal lessees (and when it becomes applicable, presumably, oil-shale lessees) for reclamation purposes,[15] the National Academy of Sciences has declared that restoration of strip-mined

Energy as landfill: Pyramid Canyon, Colorado, which may be buried under the sooty residue from processed oil shale.

coal lands to their original state "is not possible anywhere." The best that can be hoped for, the Academy states, is that in some cases the land can be made into a "stable ecological state that does not contribute substantially to environmental destruction and is consistent with surrounding esthetic values."

The situation with regard to oil-shale lands is no better; in fact, it is worse. It is the unique nature of oil-shale materials that after processing to remove the oil, the material occupies 25 percent more volume than it did before processing; 75 percent of that processed material, presumably, can be shoveled back into the hole from which it came, but the remaining 25 percent has to be put somewhere else. The government has been eyeing the canyons of the West speculatively; so have conservationists, who are not likely to let such a thing happen without loud and vigorous opposition. Among other things, they point out that however intricately such deposits are "terraced" or how thoroughly they are "dammed" by retaining walls, sooner or later erosion will carry them into the streams and rivers of the West. Moreover, the spent shale material is a wasted, sterile stuff, loaded with salts and incapable of supporting even the slightest vegetation without heavy fertilizing, mixing with topsoils, watering, and constant hand care. No matter how rigorous our standards, no matter how sincere industry's efforts (and we have no real evidence to indicate any particular dedication on the part of the corporations), the land obviously is going to remain scarred and ripped and torn for generations before the processes of geology can wear away the damage.

And what, then, of the society this grand new industry will create? It will be, quite simply, an industrial society. One estimate has it that for every 5,000 acres of oil-shale land that is leased, as much as an additional 10,000 acres will be needed to house workers, establish supportive facilities, and build roads. Towns will bloom and boom. Much of the coal that will be mined will be used to fuel the planned phalanx of fifty immense power plants that will march across the land from the high plains to the Southwest, bringing with them more workers, more service industries, more railroad spurs, more highways, more of everyone and everything, including air pollution similar to that flowing from the Four Corners Power Plant in New Mexico.

It has already started. Rifle, Colorado, in the heart of the oil-shale country, was invaded by a small army of real estate speculators within days of the first oil-shale lease bid in January 1974. The price of houses has nearly doubled, and subdividable agricultural land is going for as much as $10,000 an acre. The town's present population of about 2,500 is expected to bloat to more than 20,000 when the oil-shale development gets under way. Traffic jams have become a daily occurrence in Rock Springs, Wyoming, where the new Jim Bridger Power Plant is being built; the town's population has jumped from 12,000 in 1970 to more than 26,000 today; crime has increased, the incidence of alcoholism is on the rise, the town is surrounded on all sides by house trailers and campers, and the director of the Chamber of Commerce fears for the future: "We're just plain going crazy now. What would happen if we ever doubled *again*?"

Rock Springs may well double again. So may many other towns in this newest West, some of them not even in existence yet. The price of progress goes on and on. It has always taken its toll of the land. Now, driven by the hunger of the East and the Far West for fuel and for power, it will take its toll of those who call the land home. The country of the Big Sky has been put on the auction block.

XI

ONCE UPON AN ARROW

PERHAPS THE MOST CONSISTENT LOSERS in the lottery known as the American Dream have been the country's first immigrants—the Indians. The long, sorry tale of the culture clash that turned their world upside down is too familiar to discuss in any detail here, save to remark that it is a kind of miracle that any Indians at all remain. "It is the nature of human ecology," anthropologist John Greenway has written, "that hunting-gathering and Neolithic peoples cannot survive against the onslaughts of expanding agriculturists. The fact that the Indians—and especially the Plains Indians, who upon their acquisition of the horse reverted to a hunting-gathering subsistence—managed to save not only their populating viability but also their pride and their culture, is a tribute to the psychic energy that made them and motivated them."

The United States Census for 1970 recorded the living presence of 791,839 Indians in this country. The Indians survive, but they survive at the lowest level of American society, trapped there by two centuries of a paradox that lies at the core of American life. We are certainly not the first highly developed agricultural people to have overrun the lands occupied by a marginal subsistence culture, but we may well be the first people in history to have assumed a burden of guilt because of it. Even as the first powerful thrust of the westward movement was filling up the valley of the Mississippi with expanding agriculturists, President James Monroe could lament the fate of the Indians in 1818: "The progress of our settlements westward, supported as they are by a dense population, has constantly driven them back, with almost the total sacrifice of the lands which they have been compelled to abandon. They have claims on the magnanimity and I may add, on the justice of this

209

nation which we must all feel. We should become their real benefactors. . . . "

That sentiment, expressing at least a theoretical benevolent paternalism, was absorbed into the bloodstream of the growing beast we soon came to recognize as bureaucracy. Yet the sentiment was the child of an Eastern environment, where the Indian "problem" was almost an abstraction. Out on the cutting edge of the frontier it was no abstraction; it was a reality whose raw and sometimes bloody outlines could not be softened by rhetoric. The Indians occupied the land; the frontier wanted the land, demanded the land, would not be denied the land. And as the westward movement grew in force and political significance; its desires not only could not be ignored, they had to be accommodated if the nation itself were to survive. The government in Washington found itself in the dilemma of having to do what its highest ideals said it could not do—dispossess an entire race of people. Therein lay the paradox. Paradox begat confusion, and confusion has ever since fed the roots of official Indian policy in the United States, an amalgam of guilt, greed, promises, broken promises, and a desperate inability to reconcile the forces of history and conscience. "That the Indian is confused in mind as to his status and very much at sea as to our ultimate purpose toward him, is not surprising," Interior Secretary Franklin K. Lane wrote in 1914. "For a hundred years he has been spun around like a blindfolded child in a game of blindman's bluff. Treated as an enemy at first, overcome, driven from his lands, negotiated with most formally as an independent nation, given by treaty a distinct boundary which was never to be changed 'while water runs and grass grows,' he later found himself pushed beyond that boundary line, negotiated with again, and then set down upon a reservation, half captive, half protegé. What could an Indian, simple thinking and direct of mind, make of all this? . . . To him it must have seemed the systematized malevolence of a cynical civilization. . . . Manifestly, the Indian has been confused in his thought because we have been confused in ours."

The confusion continues, and because of it Indians today are the least well-fed, the least well-housed, the least well-educated, the least healthy, and the least employed minority group in the United States. None of the solutions offered by the government in the past or in the present has done much to bring him out of this abyss of poverty, and since this is an age of activism and ethnic assertiveness, it should not be surprising to see the Indian—like the black and Chicano before him—begin presenting his own solutions. Nor should it be surprising, since the Indian is quite as human as the white man whose victim he has been, to find that at least one of those solutions is caught in the net of yet another confusion.

The particular solution offered is land, perhaps as much as 110 million acres to serve as a land base for Indian survival, some of it to be carved out of existing national parks and forests, but most of it out of the public domain remaining in the lower forty-eight states, land owned by *all* American citizens—including the Indian. First widely promulgated by Kirke Kickingbird and Karen Ducheneaux in *One Hundred Million Acres* (1973), the basis of the demand is the same that has activated the proceedings of the Indian Claims Commission, established in 1946—the conviction that many Indian tribes have legitimate claims on land out of which they were cheated or from which they were driven in the nineteenth century. Up until recently, the bulk of the claims have been recompensed in money, but there is a growing sentiment among many Indians and those who support them that payment should be in land, not money. Even so, most of the 580 individual claims have been settled by the commission—to the tune of some $400 million as of April, 1973.

The militant American Indian Movement (AIM), founded in 1968 and notable for its participation in the seizure of the Bureau of Indian Affairs building in Washington in November of 1972 and the second battle of Wounded Knee in February and March of 1973, carried a twenty-point proposal to Washington by the "Trail of Broken Treaties Caravan" in November 1972, and in the document articulated its land-base demand: "The next Congress and Administration should commit themselves and effect a national commitment, implemented by statutes or executive and administrative actions, to restore a permanent non-diminishing Native American land base of not less than 110 million acres by July 4, 1976. This land base and its separate parts, should be vested with the recognized rights and conditions of being perpetually non-taxable, except by autonomous and sovereign Indian authority, and should never again be permitted to be alienated from Native American or Indian ownership and control."

It might be tempting to dismiss AIM's 110-million-acre proposal as little more than another example of radical excess, to be taken no more seriously than black nationalist demands for a separate nation were once taken. Unfortunately, the temptation begins to dissipate in the light of several facts: that a minority plank supporting the allocation of federal surplus lands to Indians on a first-priority basis passed by a voice vote punctuated by war whoops during the Democratic National Convention of 1972; that a judge involved in the still unsettled claim of the Pit River Indians of northern California for 3.4 million acres (including most of Lassen National Park and Forest) has commented that "These Indians may very well file suit for ownership to that land and win it"; that the Indians of the Taos Pueblo of New Mexico were given 48,000 acres of Carson National Forest in 1971; that the Havasupai Tribe of Arizona were given 185,000 acres of Grand Canyon National Park and Monument and Kaibab National Forest by Congress in December, 1974; and finally, that the Indians, Aleuts, and Eskimos of Alaska were in fact allotted no less than *40 million acres* with the Native Claims Settlement Act of 1971.

The threat is real. But while legitimately pointing out the vagueness of the AIM proposal, the response of the Nixon administration apparently misunderstood its scope: "The Federal government now holds in trust about 40 million acres of tribal land owned in common, plus approximately ten million acres of land held in trust for individual tribal members. In addition, the title to 40 million acres has been confirmed by the Congress as belonging to Alaska natives. . . . Assuming the above land is included in the suggested 110 million acre land base, this proposal calls for giving to Indians an additional 20 million acres of land. But what is omitted is the fact that claims concerning some of this additional land (it is difficult to know how much since the 110 million acres are not identified) are undoubtably [sic] involved in . . . cases now pending before the Indian Claims Commission."

The government's assumption was wrong, for if AIM spokesmen are to be believed, the demanded 110 million acres are *in addition* to the 90 million acres now conceded to the Indians and Alaska Natives, bringing the total claim to 200 million acres, all from the public domain, the *national* inheritance. If we allow this land to become a hostage to confusion, neither the Indian, the land, nor our posterity will benefit. And there is confusion involved, a confusion buried in three assumptions whose flaws have evidently escaped detection.

The first of those assumptions is that any given tribe of Indians has a claim on any given piece of land by right of prior occupancy. Strictly speaking, the legal validity of such a claim remains open to debate. Those who recognize its validity point to the Treaty of Fort Stanwix of 1784, which ceded lands to the Six Nations, and to similar treaties concluded with various tribes throughout the

The Titan in Fishers' Towers, a geological upthrust found near Moab, Utah.

nineteenth century. Those who question the legality of those treaties argue that the Ordinances of 1785 and 1787 legally precluded turning over these lands to "foreign powers," even if those powers happened to be American Indians.

But whether the Indians' current claims are strictly legal or not, they do, rightly or wrongly, possess a certain moral authority with many Americans. Recognizing this, those making such claims invariably assume the highest moral tones, implying that the appropriation of Indian lands by white society was a callous act unprecedented on the North American continent—an act unique to white society. This tone, which plays upon the strings of our guilt, enforces the Indian's contention that he has a moral as well as a legal claim to the land. "The Indians just want their land back," AIM leader Barrie Caldwell has said. "I know if I owed the white man something, he would come and take it back. The Indian is tired of being ripped off and he wants his land back."

Quite apart from the fact that land ownership was a concept alien to most Indian societies in the United States, this presumption of morality deserves examination, for it suggests a static condition among Indian societies at the time of European intrusion, a system of neatly carved up and uncontested plots of land held in peace and relative prosperity by sundry "nations" of Indians, a system disrupted and finally destroyed by white society. In fact, the Indian civilizations of the North American continent—like most civilizations on most continents in the world—had been in an almost perpetual state of flux since prehistoric times, constantly mingling cultures and languages, migrating, expanding, contracting, vanishing, fighting one another for hunting territory, agricultural territory, trade territory, or slave territory. It was a condition accelerated but by no means instituted by the appearance of Europeans on this continent.

In such a context, the concept of prior occupancy takes on elements of the absurd and claims of moral ascendency evaporate like summer rain. If the descendents of nineteenth-century white Americans have a moral obligation to the descendents of nineteenth-century Navajos, do not the Navajos have a similar obligation to the descendents of the Pueblo Indians, whom they forced from their lands in the thirteenth century? If white Americans have a moral obligation to the Chippewas (or Ojibways), do not the Chippewas have a moral obligation to the Dakota Sioux, whose lands they appropriated by warfare in the seventeenth century? If white Americans have a moral obligation to the Blackfeet, do not the Blackfeet have a moral obligation to the Shoshoni, who were driven out of their hunting territory by the Blackfeet in the seventeenth century? If white Americans have a moral obligation to the Cherokees, do not the Cherokees have a moral obligation to the Shawnees, whom they vanquished in the early nineteenth century in a war over which tribe would have a monopoly on selling Indian slaves to the South? Morality is a notoriously tricky proposition, and if we concede that Indians have a legal claim on compensation for lands appropriated by white society, it does not necessarily follow that they have a moral claim on the land itself—land that belongs to all Americans.

The second assumption, which by now has acquired the unquestioned validity of gospel, is that by instinct, training, and tradition the American Indian is a superior steward of the land, and that by giving it over into his care we may actually be saving it from the unique depredations of white society. The Indian, some have gone so far as to say, was the "first ecologist," and historian Alvin M. Josephy, Jr. has written that many Indians "yet feel a sacred attachment to the land and a reverence for nature that is incomprehensible to most whites. Many, though Christian, find repugnance in the idea that man possesses dominion over the birds and beasts, and believe still man is brother to all else that is living."

No one with eyes to see or ears to hear is going to argue that the impact of white society on the American environment has been anything less than a disaster. Nor is it reasonable to deny that in its purest form the Indian's relationship to the land displayed a sense of balance and respect that would indeed be incomprehensible to most whites. The Indian, in fact, had little choice, for in the hard game of survival he was forced by circumstances to play, respect—even reverence—for the rules of nature was often a life-or-death proposition. Men tend to make gods of those things in their world that will propitiate disaster or promote security, and the Indian quite literally worshipped much of the land around him; it was the land that nurtured him. (That attitude, obviously, even if there is as much fear as love in it, is something we could cultivate to our profit today.)

Even then, however, many Indians exhibited a certain dionysian carelessness that led them into some pretty curious ecological practices. Near Augusta, Montana, for example, there is a line of cliffs known as a *pikun*, or "Jumping-Off Place." At the foot of those cliffs is a long pile of buffalo bones, the remains of animals driven off for purposes of food, clothing, and all the other things the Plains Indians derived from the buffalo, their most sacred animal. Archeologists estimate the collection to represent at least 500,000 buffalo, most of them destroyed before European contact. Such examples of overkill (and there are others) have led some historians to conclude that even if the white man had never arrived, the buffalo would have been exterminated. Combine that human carelessness with the equally human temptations of wealth and power, and the Indian was frequently willing, even eager, to alter the fragile balance on which his very survival depended. It was Indians, after all, who stripped many fur-bearing animals from the Northeast woodlands, the Great Lakes region, and the Ohio Valley in the seventeenth and eighteenth centuries in exchange for guns, knives, whiskey, and other gewgaws of the Iron Age; it was Indians who cheerfully participated in a similar fur trade in the trans-Mississippi West in the first half of the nineteenth century; and it was Indians who contributed to the stunningly swift annihilation of the great buffalo herds of the plains in the last half of the nineteenth century, again in exchange for those tools of progress they hoped would increase their power and prosperity.

Today, the sense of a necessary balance between man and nature remains strong among many Indian peoples, as Josephy noted, but it would be fruitless to maintain that that sense is universal or that it characterizes modern Indian use of Indian land. One spectacular piece of evidence, of course, is the profound overgrazing on the Navajo reservation. Between 1870 and 1935 the Navajo (who had been shepherds for nearly two hundred years) managed to overstock their range by more than 200 percent; when the Indian Service attempted to institute a stock reduction program, the Indians resisted bitterly, in spite of increasing and visible damage to the land. Stock reduction was finally and painfully achieved over the years, but for much of the land it was too late. A similar situation exists on the Paiute reservation of northwestern Nevada, where rampant overgrazing has reduced the land on the east shore of Pyramid Lake to a windblown Sahara that is often downright dangerous to drive. On the lower Colorado River, Indian land has been turned over to cheapjack developers of summer homes and housing projects. In eastern Montana and the Southwest eleven coal strip-mining leases have been granted to private companies by Indian tribal councils; the average size of these leases covers 23,523 acres, fifteen times larger than similar leases on public lands, and the Bureau of Indian Affairs, according to the Council on Economic Priorities, has displayed an "abysmal record" in enforcing environmental guidelines and restrictions.

Overgrazing, strip mining, resort development, clear cutting on Northwest timber lands . . . none of this is to suggest that the

The marks of America's first immigrants, gentler than those modern Indians might well inflict on the land, are scattered throughout the West. Above, petroglyphs in an undisclosed canyon; below, in Arches National Monument.

Indian is any more inclined to misuse the land than his counter-
parts in the white world, only that he has shown in more than one
instance that he can. Generally speaking, the Indian's concept of
success is in terms of the whole community's success, whereas the
white man thinks of success in terms of individual opportunity.
The Indian's attitude may be much the superior, one from which
white society could learn a good deal. Yet when the Indian community demonstrates itself quite as capable of inflicting wreckage
on the environment as any gimlet-eyed practitioner of free enterprise, the point becomes irrelevant to the question of land use.
Irrelevant, simply because it is the larger community of life that is
damaged by both.

The third and final assumption involved in the Indian's demand for land is that its possession will in some magical way solve
the material problems of a century. That is a seductive vision. It
speaks of many things important to him, of freedom from the
stifling bureaucracy that has trammeled his existence since he
became a ward of the government, of escape from the poverty and
ignorance that has kept him out of the sun like a man trapped in a
closet, of the chance to stand and be considered an equal in a world
whose history has passed him by, of the dream of maintaining the
best of the lifeways of his fathers. It is also a delusion, if the lessons of
the past have any meaning. The largest and one of the oldest Indian
reservations is that of the Navajo. Established in 1868, it now comprises more than 25,000 square miles. That is a lot of land, enough
to make the reservation a shade larger than the state of West Virginia. It is not enough land and has never been enough land to keep
its more than 100,000 people as a whole much above the bottom
line of poverty. A land base, as any squint-eyed rancher of the
northern plains or any hard-scrabble farmer of Missouri would be
quick to note, is by no means a guarantee of the good life. Most of
the land from which the demanded 110 million-acre land base
would be carved is unsuited for agriculture. Grazing land, even if
properly managed, will not support large numbers of people, nor
will timber lands. Modern metals mining, operating on a high-
investment, low-return basis, is a shaky business for even the most
sophisticated corporation.

Even strip-mining leases, the latest entry in the energy-
exploitation sweepstakes, are not calculated to raise individual income levels to the national average. For example, the Navajo tribe's
share of the royalties from Peabody Coal Company's two Black
Mesa leases (13 million tons a year at 25 cents a ton divided with
the Hopi tribe) will amount to an additional $16.25 for each of the

reservation's 100,000 residents. Increase the coal output tenfold, and individual income would rise $162.50; increase it a hundred-fold, and income would rise to $1,625—while the mesa would sink to become a hole in the ground.

Land as a viable solution to the economic needs of the Indian is a demonstrable myth. There are simply too many Indians and too little land available for a reasonable economic return, even if all the stops were pulled and the Indian was allowed to graze it down to the roots, strip it clean of timber, pockmark it with strip mines, sell it to every interested developer, use it up, wear it out, kill it dead.

Flawed assumptions: if land is not the solution, what is? The answer—though not its implications—is a simple one, which can be applied equally to all the varieties of minority-group situations in the United States. For the first time in its history, this country must come to terms with the fact that in 200 years it has not come close to fulfilling its highest ideals, has not in fact provided equal opportunity under the law, has not put its heart, mind, and money into a wholesouled effort to find social solutions to social problems. In our social structure, as in our technological structure, we are racing toward the end of this century at frightening speed, very nearly out of control; if we do not soon gain that control, we are less likely to become a nation of people than a nation of bickering factions of haves and have-nots squabbling over the last bone in the pot. The American Indian, the gadfly in our souls for 200 years, lost for all that time in the paradox of the American Dream, must be led out of confusion—ours as well as his—by *action*, not by spurious giveaways of the American land, meaningless gestures that give him nothing while depriving the generations to come of a good part of their legacy.

That legacy must be shared by all. "We Indians say 'our country,'" John Fire/Lame Deer, a holy man of the Lakota Sioux wrote in 1972, "because it is still ours even if all other races are now in physical possession of it, for land does not belong to any single man but to all people and to the future generations. We must try to use the pipe for mankind, which is on the road to self-destruction. . . . This can be done only if all of us, Indians and non-Indians alike, can again see ourselves as part of this earth, not as an enemy from the outside who tries to impose his will on it. Because we, who know the meaning of the pipe, also know that, being a living part of the earth, we cannot harm any part of her without hurting ourselves. . . . Through this pipe, maybe, we can make peace with our greatest enemy, who dwells deep within us."

EPILOGUE

AS THESE WORDS ARE WRITTEN, it is March 15, 1975. The country wallows in the mire of the worst recession—possibly depression—within the memory of those under forty years of age. Financial experts scrabble through the ashes of the economy looking for solutions like Indian bone-pickers sifting out the remains of their ancestors. Congress and the Ford-Rockefeller administration squabble over cause and effect, blame and credit, problems and programs, like surgeons bickering in the operating room while the patient slowly wastes away. In his "Doonesbury" comic strip, Gary Trudeau features a radio interview program during which two economists announce that the country is doomed and proceed to mug the announcer.

The country may not be doomed, but it is most certainly confused. And, as in all confusions, something is likely to be lost sight of along the way. At this writing, that something appears to be a whole raft of environmental problems, and not the least of these by any means is the question of the future of the American public domain. The fine flush of enthusiasm that accompanied the introduction and movement of bills for its protection in the House and Senate during 1974 (however unsuccessful they turned out to be) seems to have dissipated more than a little. In the House, no new bills at all have been introduced. Once again, it is the Senate which has opened the question of the public domain (contrary to earlier predictions that the Senate, having been repeatedly thwarted in its efforts by the House, would take a "wait and see" attitude). Senators Haskell, Jackson, and Metcalf have introduced S. B. 507, a measure that includes many of the desirable provisions of the late lamented S. B. 524 (see Chapter 7), but whose future is questionable. Conservationists cheer that portion of the bill which repeals the various desert entry laws, but are justifiably concerned that it

221

does not repeal the General Mining Law of 1872 (although it does include clauses providing for the reclamation of land which has been mined). The administration (in the persons of Rogers C. B. Morton, Secretary of the Interior, and Curtis J. Berklund, Director of the Bureau of Land Management) has indicated its general support of the bill—with one major proviso: that those portions of it that call for a wilderness review for areas of the public domain of 5,000 acres or more be revised to stipulate that only areas of 50,000 acres or more be considered, a condition that would eliminate literally hundreds of potential wilderness areas. Conservationists regard this possibility with about as much enthusiasm as a Navajo contemplating the idea of eating fish—that is to say, none.

The grazing lands of the public domain face their own kind of problems as this book goes to press—in spite of the recent court ruling that requires the Bureau of Land Management to file detailed environmental impact statements before issuing new grazing permits (see Chapter 8 and "Notes"). Representative John Melcher, chairman of the House Subcommittee on Public Lands, has announced that hearings will be held on the question of raising the fees for grazing permits. This is a proposal much to be desired; for more than forty years, stockmen have been receiving what amounts to a federal subsidy in the ridiculously low rates charged for the use of the national lands, and it is well past the time when they should have been charged prices more in line with value received. Unfortunately, there will very likely be what Charles Clausen, one of the Sierra Club's Washington representatives, calls a "Catch-22" in the whole businss: stockmen's Congressional spokesmen (the name of Representative Samuel Steiger of Arizona comes immediately to mind) probably will support a modest increase in permit fees—but only in exchange for the issuance of ten-year permits, something which stockmen have been after ever since passage of the Taylor Grazing Act of 1934. Once again, conservationists do not welcome any such notion, believing for good and sufficient reasons that any man privileged to put his animals on the public domain should be held accountable for his use of that land on a year-to-year basis.

Altogether, the question of what we intend to do with the national lands—the greatest single resource we possess—remains in doubt, possibly no closer to a resolution now than it was when Congress first began to explore possibilities in 1964. One of the major obstacles in the way of hammering out some kind of intelligent management program, unhappily, comes from the highest levels of the very agency created to administer and protect the public domain: the Bureau of Land Management. There appears to be—to put it mildly—a certain lack of interest in anything but a purely utilitarian use of these lands by BLM Director, Curtis J. Berklund, and he seems to be supported in his attitudes by his employer, Rogers C. B. Morton, who has become particularly entranced by the energy potential they may harbor. As a result, there is a growing sentiment among many conservationists for the creation of a brand-new agency to assume the responsibilities of the Bureau of Land Management—possibly under the aegis of the Department of Agriculture. Not even those who have given voice to such a proposal truly believe that it has much chance of being translated into law, but at the very least it articulates a frustration quite as real as it is lamentable. In this case, it would seem, revolution is going to have to begin at the top.

That revolution is not going to take place without the same public support that has helped to engineer every major piece of environmental legislation in recent years. Congress, as more than one observer has noted, is not a self-starting machine; its ignition key is the public. We must turn that key, and turn it now. If we do not, if we allow history to repeat itself, we will have abandoned our primary inheritance. More importantly, we will have turned our backs on our responsibility to all those who must follow us—our children, our childrens' children, their children, and all the generations of children lost in the distances beyond our own mortality.

APPENDICES

A NOTE ON SOURCES

Given the importance of the subject to a proper understanding of the American narrative, it is somewhat astonishing that there have been only two major histories of the public domain published for a general audience in recent years: *Our Landed Heritage: The Public Domain, 1776–1936*, by Roy M. Robbins (Princeton, New Jersey, 1942), and *The Closing of the Public Domain*, by Louise Peffer (Palo Alto, California, 1951). The Robbins book is particularly valuable for its discussion of the sectional rivalries that accompanied the development of public-land laws throughout most of the nineteenth century and for its treatment of the years of the two administrations of Theodore Roosevelt; after that the book becomes increasingly general and is especially weak in regard to the forces and ideas that resulted in passage of the Taylor Grazing Act. That shortcoming is remedied superbly in Louise Peffer's book, which lays bare with a cool precision the seemingly endless conflict between the special interest of the stockman and the general interest of the public.

A succinct and scholarly approach to the subject is presented in *The History of Public Land Law Development*, by Paul W. Gates and Robert W. Swensen (Government Printing Office, 1968), a report written for (but without the prejudices of) Wayne Aspinall's Public Land Law Review Commission. A. M. Sakolski's *The Great American Land Bubble* (New York, 1927), while by no means a proper history of the public domain, is useful for its discussion of sundry frauds and speculations, particularly for the years preceding, during, and immediately following the Revolution. A necessarily general, but nonetheless well-orchestrated treatment of the public domain and its importance to the westward movement is found in Ray Allen Billington's *Westward Expansion* (New York, 1973). In *Virgin Land: The American West as Symbol and Myth* (Cambridge, Massachusetts, 1950) Henry Nash Smith has illuminated the literary and emotional attitudes that helped shape our use of the American land.

In more specific areas, Walter Prescott Webb's *The Great Plains* (Boston, 1931) remains the classic study of America's somewhat uncertain approach to the land that stretched west from the Mississippi and Missouri rivers to the Rocky Mountains; also indispensable, though more concerned with the nature of the land than with the nature of those who came to take it from the wind, is James C. Malin's *Grasslands of North America* (Lawrence, Kansas, 1947). The seminal land-use theories of Major John Wesley Powell have been given their most informed expression in *Beyond the Hundredth Meridian: John Wesley Powell and the Second Opening of the West*, by Wallace Stegner (Boston, 1954). The story of the use, abuse, and rescue of the timberlands of the public domain is presented with much style by Richard G. Lillard's *The Great Forest* (New York, 1947) and with a tinge of understandable prejudice by Gifford Pinchot's autobiography, *Breaking New Ground* (New York, 1947). In Chapter 6 of *The Lands No One Knows*, "Two-Gun Desmond and the Paradox Factor," I have relied heavily on Bernard DeVoto, especially the collection of essays he gathered into *The Easy Chair* (Boston, 1955), and on Wallace Stegner's splendid biography of DeVoto, *The Uneasy Chair* (New York, 1974).

Since any history of the public domain must be in a very real sense a history of the West itself, it would be fruitless to list all of the numerous sources that were inevitably and regularly consulted beyond those mentioned above. Personal preference, however, enjoins me to single out the following for special mention: *The Indian Heritage of America*, by Alvin M. Josephy, Jr. (New York, 1968); *The Sod-House Frontier, 1854–1890*, by Everett Dick (New York, 1937); *The Day of the Cattleman*, by Ernest A. Osgood (St. Paul, Minnesota, 1929); *Mining Frontiers of the Far West, 1848–1880*, by Rodman Paul (New York, 1963); and *The Great Persuader: A Biography of Collis P. Huntington*, by David Lavender (New York, 1970).

Finally, as noted in the preface to this book, the single most important source of materials for my discussion of the modern public domain and its problems was the substantial collection of papers maintained by Charles S. Watson, Jr. for the Nevada Outdoor Recreation Association and the National Public Lands Task Force. These have been supplemented, where necessary, by materials from the files of the Sierra Club and the Bureau of Land Management, and by interviews with Bureau officials and conservationists.

T. H. WATKINS

NOTES

1. It should be mentioned here that the federal government acquired no public-domain land with the addition of Texas. In a unique departure from tradition, the Texas Annexation Resolution of March 1, 1845, stipulated that "Said state, when admitted into the Union . . . shall also retain all the vacant and unappropriated lands lying within its limits."

2. Some idea of the largesse available through a diligent application of the homestead, timber-culture, and desert-land laws may be gained from the following hypothesis: suppose a relatively modest cattle outfit was run by a man, his wife, a son, and a daughter (both over the age of twenty-one), and had a working crew of twelve hands. If each member of the family and each cowboy filed under the three laws, that outfit could accumulate no less than 15,360 acres of public lands. It is of such stuff that empires are made, and it should come as no surprise to learn that dozens of cattle operations were not "outfits," but baronies comprising hundreds of thousands of acres.

3. The last provision of the 1897 legislation, called the Forest Lieu Land Act, was not only a sop but a boon to railroad interests, who were now able to dump marginally profitable or totally unprofitable grant lands and "relocate" them where it would do the most good —for them. In this way, the Southern Pacific Railroad, for example, exchanged desert lands in Nevada and Utah for lieu lands in the spectacularly fertile San Joaquin Valley of California. Small wonder that Western railroads became active supporters of additional forest reserves, an embarrassment to the conservation movement that was overcome when the Lieu Land Act was repealed in 1905.

4. The proposed amendment: "No renewal of any such permit shall be denied, if such denial will impair the value of the livestock unit of the permittee, if such unit is pledged as security for any bona fide loan." Such bona fide loans, of course, could be so small as to be nearly invisible—cheap insurance for what would amount to a lifetime permit to graze the public land.

5. Since the specious constitutional argument continues to pop up from time to time even today, we might as well deal with it here. Its proponents point to Subsection 17 of Article I, Section 8 of the Constitution, which deals with the powers of Congress, one of these being to "exercise exclusive legislation in all cases whatsoever over such district (not exceeding ten square miles) as may, by cession of particular states and the acceptance of Congress, become the seat of government [i.e., the District of Columbia] of the United States and

to exercise like authority over all plaçes purchased, by the consent of the legislature of the state in which the same shall be, for the erection of forts, magazines, arsenals, dockyards, and other needful buildings." Ah, ha! these strict constructionists cry, the seat of government, forts, magazines, arsenals, dockyards, and other needful buildings—but nothing about national parks, national forests, or Taylor Act grazing lands. Clearly such reserves are unconstitutional, for nothing in our national document authorizes the federal government to own or administer any lands other than those stipulated in Article I. Well, yes, as a matter of fact, there is something—namely, Subsection 2 of Article IV, Section 3, which declares that "The Congress shall have the power to dispose of and make all needful rules and regulations, respecting the territory or other property belonging to the United States; and nothing in this Constitution shall be construed as to prejudice any claim of the United States, or of any particular state." Obviously written to legitimize the cession of Western lands to the United States in 1780 and the ordinances of 1785 and 1787, this provision gives the federal government all the authority it needs. Further, the Supreme Court upheld that authority in 1917 with its decision in the case of the U.S. *vs.* the Utah Power & Light Company (see Chapter 5). And finally, as Bernard DeVoto pointed out, any Westerner who maintains that government possession of land is unconstitutional had better start wondering just who will guarantee the title to any Western land he might own; if the government did not have the right to own, sell, or dispose of it under the various land laws, then his possession is quite illegal—he is, in fact, a squatter.

6. The words of Dr. Hudson are sadly reminiscent of those of Charles C. Moore almost precisely twenty years before, uttered after attendance at one of Congressman Frank Barrett's 1947 subcommittee hearings—"Stockman Barrett's Wild West Show," as it was called by the Denver *Post*. "I have sat through dreary hours," Moore said then, "listening to repetition, testimony of personal problems, testimony filled with useless verbiage; of the approximately fifteen hours of testimony, less than one hour and one-half was accorded our side for discussion of matters supposed to be taken up . . . . Never in all my experience have I attended a meeting so one-sided and unfair, so full of bias." This, as well as many other aspects of Barrett's hearings, was delightfully analyzed by Bernard DeVoto in "Sacred Cows and the Public Lands" in *The Easy Chair* (1955).

7. The stockmen are aided and abetted by intermountain banks and other lending institutions, who consider grazing permits tantamount to land ownership and treat them as collateral in granting loans—a condition that accelerates the growth of corporate stock raising by encouraging steady, if not particularly intelligent, expansion: the

more permits you can get, the more loans you can get; the more loans you can get, the more permits you can get; and so on, *ad infinitum, ad absurdum*.

8. In fact, Hickel was inclined to favor outright disposal—as suggested by his participation in the Point Reyes Exchange Program of 1969 to 1970, which would have exchanged as much as 770,000 acres of Nevada public-domain land for the few hundred acres of privately owned land on Point Reyes needed to fill out the boundaries of California's national seashore. Before public opinion stifled the program (oral and written testimony at a public hearing in Nevada, for example, resulted in 22 items of testimony in favor of the exchange and 10,058 items against it), Hickel had approved of 14,420 acres for disposal in exchange for only 22 acres of Point Reyes land; most of this exchange land went to a clique of five Nevada ranchers who had foresightedly purchased the Point Reyes land—and represented an exchange ration of 655 acres to 1.

9. Any notion that these words represented any real change in Nixon's feelings was dispelled on July 25, 1972, according to an Associated Press story of that date. Speaking to his Federal Property Review Board, the president pointed to a large map of the United States and announced that the government owned half the land. "That's ridiculous," he said. "We don't need it." He also complained that "Agencies seem to get a vested interest in every piece of land they have and they fight against turning it over." *Sic transit* rhetoric.

10. As of January 1975, many of these local boards in several Western states were scheduled for dissolution, and the Bureau of Land Management planned to create new ones containing broader representation of legitimate land users. Stockmen, unsurprisingly, announced that they would attempt to block any such move.

11. On December 30, 1974, in a decision that surprised conservationists quite as much as it appalled stockmen, the U.S. District Court upheld the suit, declaring among other things, that "The court is aware that, like many agencies, the BLM has been given large scale tasks to be accomplished with limited manpower. That does not mean, however, that the agency may ignore or pay mere lip service to the NEPA requirements." The government has since decided that it will not appeal the decision, but stockmen, acting as "intervenor–defendants," have announced that they will—as long and as far as necessary.

12. One such move for conciliation has been made by the singularly militant Nevada Outdoor Recreation Association, which has been advocating the creation of an "adventure road" system for four-wheel-drive vehicles on specified areas of the public domain that

already possess dirt roads and tracks. Since 1967 the suggestion has in fact been implemented by the Bureau of Land Management in several districts throughout the West.

13. A 1974 amendment to the Sikes Act of several years ago expanded that act's authority to include the regulation of off-road vehicle use on Department of Defense lands. Many conservationists believe that this amendment, if properly interpreted, gives the Bureau of Land Management the power to regulate vehicles on the public domain. The Bureau apparently does not agree—it recommended the veto of the 1974 amendment—and the question remains unresolved at this writing.

14. Interior Secretary Stewart Udall had attempted to institute such a program as early as 1967 by announcing the availability of lease sites. There were no takers—not simply because there was no "crisis" in those good old days, but because the price of oil and gasoline was not high enough to interest the companies in expanding their production through oil-shale development.

15. This "strip-mining bill" was pocket-vetoed by President Gerald Ford in December 1974 on the grounds that it would lead to an inflationary rise in the price of coal—even though he had been warned by friend and foe alike that the more conservation-minded 94th Congress would be likely to enact even stiffer legislation.

A CHRONOLOGY OF MAJOR PUBLIC-LAND LAWS

1780

At the request of the Continental Congress, New York cedes all its Western land claims to the new government of the United States. Massachusetts follows suit in 1784, Connecticut in 1786, South Carolina in 1787, North Carolina in 1790, and Georgia in 1802. All of these lands, collectively, constitute the original public domain.

1785

Land Ordinance establishes a rectangular system of cadastral surveys of public lands in the Northwest Territory north of the Ohio River. This system divides public lands into townships of six square miles and each township into thirty-six sections of 640 acres each. Five sections of each township are to be reserved, the remaining thirty-one to be disposed of at auctions held in each of the original thirteen states—in blocks of no less than 640 acres and at a minimum price of $1.00 per acre.

1787

Northwest Ordinance provides a basis for the territorial self-government of settlers who have migrated to the land north of the Ohio River; future new states in that region will be admitted to the Union on equal terms with the original states.

1796

Act of May 18 raises minimum price per acre for public lands to $2.00 and stipulates that half of such lands shall be sold in tracts of 5,760 acres each. Act also establishes the trans-Appalachian West's first local land offices, at Pittsburgh and Cincinnati.

1800

Act of May 10 retains minimum public-land sale price of $2.00, but reduces the minimum unit of sale to only 320 acres and establishes a credit system of four annual payments.

1804

Act of March 26 reduces minimum land-sale unit to 160 acres and the purchase price to $1.64 per acre.

1812

Act of April 25 creates the General Land Office under the Treasury Department. Duties of office include issuance of land warrants and grants, schedule of sales at various district land offices, collection of money from sales, preparation and issuance of patents or deeds, and maintenance of land records. General Land Office abolished in 1946.

1820

Act of April 24 abandons the credit system for the purchase of public lands. Minimum price is fixed at $1.25 per acre and unit size reduced to 80 acres.

1830

Congress passes the first Pre-emption Act, which entitles any settler on the unsurveyed public domain to claim any number of acres up to a maximum of 160 and buy it from the government for $1.25 per acre. Act due to expire in two years, but renewed in 1832, 1834, 1838, and 1840.

1841

Pre-emption Act extended indefinitely, not to be revoked until 1891.

1849

Act of March 3 creates the Department of the Interior; General Land Office is taken out of the Treasury Department and put under the supervision of the new department.

1850

Act of September 20 grants public lands to aid in the construction of the Illinois Central Railroad and the Mobile & Ohio Railroad. Swamp Lands Act of the same year grants all "swamp and overflow" lands in the states to the states; proceeds from the state sale of such lands are to be used for their reclamation.

1854

Graduation Act authorizes the periodic reduction in the price of unsold lands, price determined by the length of time land has been on the market.

1862

Homestead Act allows unrestricted settlement on public lands to all settlers, requiring only the residence, improvement, and cultivation of a tract of 160 acres. Any person twenty-one years old or the head of a household is eligible, as are aliens who have declared their intention to become citizens. After living on and farming the land for six months, the settler can buy it for $1.25 per acre; or he can live on it for five continuous years and then receive a patent or title for the payment of a small filing fee. Pacific Railroad Act in this year grants both federal loans and tracts of public land to the Central Pacific Railroad and the Union Pacific Railroad to aid in the construction of a transcontinental railroad. Also, Morrill Land Grant Act is passed, authorizing the grant of public lands to individual states to support the development of state vocational colleges teaching agriculture and the mechanical arts.

1872

General Mining Law throws open all public lands to private prospecting and development. Patent can be obtained by making a valid mineral discovery, investing $100 in improvements annually for five years, paying for a boundary survey, applying to a land office for the land included in such boundary, and paying $2.50 an acre for placer mining and $5.00 an acre for lode mining.

1873

Timber Culture Act grants an additional 160 acres of land to homesteaders who promise to plant 40 acres of the added land in trees; acreage requirements later reduced to ten acres.

1877

Desert Land Act makes 640-acre tracts of arid lands available; settler can claim tentative title to this land by first paying 25 cents an acre for it and full title by paying an additional $1.00 an acre when he can prove that he has "brought water" to the claim.

1878

Timber and Stone Act authorizes the negotiated sale of public lands unfit for cultivation but valuable for timber and stone resources. Act is repealed in 1955.

1879

A Public Lands Commission is created by Congress to assess the condition of the nation's public lands and suggest areas of possible reform in land use and disposition.

1885

Act of February 25 makes unlawful the use of any force, threats, or intimidation against settlers on the public domain, an attempt to control the activities of cattlemen determined to keep "nesters" off the land; act also declares it illegal to fence areas of the public domain in order to prevent or obstruct settlement.

1887

General Allotment Act diminishes Indian tribal land by granting tracts to individual Indians who choose to accept them; remainder of tribal lands will either be opened to settlement under the land laws or sold for the benefit of the appropriate tribes.

1891

General Revision Act repeals the Pre-emption Act, Timber Culture Act, and the auction sale of land; reduces the acreage limitation under the Desert Land Act from 640 to 320 acres; and section 24 of the Act—the "Forest Reserve Act"—authorizes the President of the United States to withdraw from settlement or exploitation any forest areas of the public domain which in the opinion of the Secretary of the Interior require watershed protection and timber preservation.

1897

Act of June 4 assigns responsibility to the Department of the Interior for the administration, conservation, and use of large areas of public lands with forests. Designated the "National Forest Reserves," these lands are to be surveyed, protected, and managed by the General Land Office.

1902

Reclamation (Newlands) Act establishes a system of water-development projects for the irrigation of arid lands of the public domain at federal expense; entitlement to federal water limited to individuals owning or claiming no more than 160 acres—"excess" lands to be sold within ten years after federal water becomes available.

1901

Act of February 1 transfers all national forest reserves from the Department of the Interior to the Department of Agriculture; forest reserves now designated national forests and bureau in charge of their protection called the Forest Service.

1909

Enlarged Homestead Act increases the area limitation in Western states to 320 acres of public domain, when such lands are classified as "dry-farming" lands and not susceptible to irrigation.

1910

Pickett Act authorizes the President of the United States to withdraw or reserve areas of public lands for reclamation, irrigation, or powersite purposes. Act of June 25 authorizes the president to withdraw public lands for *any* public purpose; later amended to specify that all such reserves would be open to the exploration, discovery, and development of metalliferous minerals under the General Mining Act.

1916

Stock-Raising Homestead Act increases the area limitation for homesteading to 640 acres for those public lands suitable only for the grazing of livestock; no cultivation of lands necessary, but some range improvements required.

1920

Mineral Leasing Act authorizes the federal government to lease public lands for the private extraction of oil, gas, coal, phosphate, sodium, and other minerals; lessee to pay an annual rental plus a graduated royalty on all minerals produced from such lands. In the same year the Federal Power Commission is created to control and coordinate the private development of hydroelectric power on the lands of the public domain.

1934

Taylor Grazing Act closes to indiscriminant settlement and use all remaining unreserved and unappropriated public-domain lands in ten

Western states, excluding Alaska. Act authorizes classification of public lands in order to assure proper usage, federal procedures to improve, develop, and conserve public lands, and creation of grazing districts for the use of the livestock industry under government permits and with government supervision. Division of Grazing (later, Grazing Service) established to function under the aegis of the General Land Office. All remaining public lands withdrawn from sale prior to classification.

1937

Bankhead–Jones Farm Tenant Act authorizes the federal purchase of submarginal private farming lands; owners to be relocated elsewhere and lands retired from agricultural production; some 2 million acres of such lands later transferred to the jurisdiction of the Department of the Interior.

1946

Act of July 16 creates Bureau of Land Management within the Department of the Interior; the responsibilities, functions, and personnel of both the General Land Office and the Grazing Service are to be combined and transferred to the new agency.

1953

Submerged Lands Act quitclaims to the states of Louisiana, Texas, and California all submerged lands lying from a point three miles at sea to the boundaries of the states involved. In the same year, the Outer Continental Shelf Lands Act authorizes the issuance of permits and leases for the exploration and development of mineral resources on federally owned submerged lands; to be administered by the Bureau of Land Management.

1964

Public Land Law Review Commission Act creates a body to investigate all existing statutes and regulations governing the retention, management, and disposal of public lands and to determine present and future demands on the public domain; this commission later issued a report entitled *One Third of a Nation's Land*. In the same year, the Public Land Sale Act (expired 1970) allows the sale of relatively small tracts of public land for certain specified uses, and the Classification and Multiple Use Act (also expired in 1970) directs the Bureau of Land Management to classify the public lands, determining which are suitable for disposal and which suitable for retention and management by the government under the principles of multiple use and sustained yield.

A WILDERNESS INDEX

In 1963, the Sierra Club published *The Place No One Knew: Glen Canyon on the Colorado*, one of the most spectacularly beautiful books in its Exhibit Format series. It was produced to document the wonders of a piece of the American landscape that would soon disappear beneath the waters of the government's Lake Powell. That piece of the landscape was part of the American public domain, the national inheritance of land held in trust and administered by the Bureau of Land Management. Yet not once in that otherwise splendid Sierra Club book was this fact mentioned, for a simple, if regrettable reason: not even the nation's leading conservation organization fully realized the scope and importance of America's public domain and the jewels of wilderness beauty it contained.

Much has changed in the past twelve years, so much, in fact, that the Sierra Club has since taken a major role in the effort to preserve and protect these lands. Still, the general public remains remarkably uninformed about the public domain, about either its quality or its extent. Hence the title of this book: *The Lands No One Knows*. Hence the purpose of the following listing: to give the reader some sense of the kind of land that is at stake. The list is by no means complete; a full listing would require a substantial book of its own. Consider the amounts of acreage involved in the twenty-four states in which public domain land exists (as compiled in the Government Printing Office's *Public Land Statistics*): Alabama, 544; Alaska, 299,144,900; Arizona, 12,602,068; Arkansas, 1,232; California, 15,584,931; Colorado, 8,387,163; Florida, 438; Idaho, 12,095,082; Kansas, 954; Louisiana, 1,516; Michigan, 840; Minnesota, 43,923; Mississippi, 546; Montana, 8,154,447; Nebraska, 7,884; Nevada, 48,389,569; New Mexico, 13,214,574; North Dakota, 69,501; Oklahoma, 7,301; Oregon, 15,697,452; South Dakota, 276,512; Utah, 22,741,721; Washington, 292,011; Wyoming, 17,423,785.

Out of this immense patrimony, the Bureau of Land Management has begun to identify interesting undeveloped regions which it is calling Primitive Areas. Ultimately, it may propose that many of these be reserved as Wilderness Areas. This list is far from complete—some would say that it is not even half complete—since the Bureau is a long ways removed from accomplishing a comprehensive inventory of its lands. Acreage figures appear in parentheses:

Arizona: Planet Peak (18,000); Kanab Creek–Hack's Canyon (25,000); Virgin Mts. (38,000); Horquahala Mts. (78,000); Table Top Mt. (33,000); Eagle Tail Mt. (33,000); Burro Creek (7,000); Arrastra Mt. (70,000); Rawhide (15,000); Black Mts. (75,000); Gila Box (75,000); Cactus Plain (69,000); Squaw Creek (22,000); Bill Williams Mts. (26,000).

California: Chimney Creek (8,000); Caliana Mt. (5,000); Sheep Mountain Rock (6,000); Keynot (85,000); Owlshead (161,000); Amapsoja (120,000);

Saline (120,000); Owens Peak (32,000); Coppersmith Hills (16,000); High Rock (23,000); Little High Rock (5,000); Hog Ranch (133,000); Round Mt. (32,000); Big Spring Table (60,000); Railroad Point (11,000); Garch Table (33,000); Catnip Mt. (40,000); Fish Creek Table (47,000); Badger Mt. (10,000); Blowout Mt. (25,000); Big Mountain (24,000); Mahogany Mt. (13,000); Cottonwood Canyon (6,000); Hell Creek Canyon (11,000); Timace Crater (17,000); Chamise Mt. (5,000).

Colorado: Cold Springs Breaks (23,000); Diamond Mt. Breaks (13,000); Cross Mt. (11,000); Yepmillion Butte (7,000); Brown's Canyon (10,000); Grape Creek (22,000); Beaver Creek (22,000); Black Ridge (50,000); Little Dominquez (21,000).

Idaho: Owyhee River (180,000); North Fork Owyhee (50,000); Jim Sage (25,000); Petticoat Peak (7,000); Hell's Half Acre (44,000); Ramreau–Vail Ridge (130,000); Great Point Mt. (320,000).

Montana: Arrow Creek (5,000); Twin Coulee (7,000); Wood Hawk (10,000); Carroll Coulee (4,000); Dog Creek (5,000); Big Coulee (5,000); Burnt Lodge (16,000); Seven Black Foot (18,000); Centennial Mts. (103,000); Ruby Mts. (21,000).

Nevada: South Fork Owyhee (32,000); Snowstorm Mts. (49,000); Beaver Mt. (28,000); Wilson Mt. (10,000); Rough Hills (10,000); Wildhorse Mt. (35,000); Adobe Range (76,000); Lone Mt. (49,000); Blue Lakes (29,000); Virginia Mts. (66,000); Fort Sage Mt. (19,000); Seven Lakes Mt. (6,000); Peterson Mt. (21,000); Fred's Mt. (6,000); Pah Rah Range (47,000); Park Mt. (31,000); Seaman Range (90,000); Phapoc (30,000); Hicks Station (12,000); Roberts Mt. (3,000); Cottonwood Basin (6,000); Trout Creek (5,000); Elephant Head (5,000); Manhattan (6,000); Morey (23,000).

New Mexico: Simon Canyon (2,000); Cebrolleta Mesa (6,000); Ladrones Peak (10,000); Florida Mts. (20,000); Big Hatchet Mts. (84,000); Cornulas Mts. (14,000); Alamo Hueco Mts. (35,000).

Oregon: Honeycombs (10,000); Leslie Gulch (15,000); Red Buttes (15,000); Sulphur Butte (12,000); North Fork Malhue River (7,000); Gerry Mt. (10,000); Sheep Mt. (8,000); Diablo Mt. (97,000); Fish Fin (34,000); Lost Forest (12,000); Jordan Craters (20,000); Sheepshead Mts. (60,000); Cox Butte (50,000); Abert Rim (30,000); Beaty's Butte (15,000); Fort Rock Lava Beds (36,000).

Utah: Little Rockies (109,000); Deep Creek (5,000); Red Mt. (14,000); Steamboat Mt. (8,000); Paradise Mt. (9,000); Wahitnu Kanse (185,000); House Knife (135,000); Mancos Mesa (113,000); Windgate Mesa (19,000); Nokai Dome (5,000); Slickhorn Canyon (3,000); White Canyon (15,000); Johns Canyon (8,000); Fish Creek Cliffs (200,000); Star and Marble Canyon

(12,000); Poison Sand Creek (5,000); Gold Bar (5,000); Bull Canyon (5,000); Rustler Canyon (3,000); Mineral Canyon (2,000); Behind the Rocks (6,000); Beef Basin (22,000); Dolores River (5,000); Canaan Mt. (33,000); Death Valley (60,000); Virgin Rock (20,000); Fifty-Mile Mt. (120,000); Deer Creek (170,000); Sids Mt. (65,000); Mexican Mt. (30,000); Kimball Wash–Hebe's Canyon (23,000); Desolation Canyon (121,000); Range Creek (25,000); Horseshoe Canyon (24,000); Robber's Roost–Dirty Devil (35,000).

Wyoming: Sweetwater Canyon (5,000); Scab Creek (7,000); Middle Fork Powder River (11,000); Powder River (22,000); Fourth Ration Creek (100,000).

The "Wilderness Index" below is an attempt to describe in some detail a number of areas of the public domain in ten Western states which I believe to be of outstanding value for their wilderness and aesthetic qualities. Some of these areas are included in the Bureau of Land Management's own list above; some are not (though many should be). As noted earlier, this Index is not comprehensive; for example, the lands in Alaska are not discussed, simply for reasons of space (for a survey of Alaskan lands, the reader can consult *Alaska: The Great Land*, by Peggy Wayburn and Mike Miller, published by the Sierra Club in the fall of 1974). However incomplete, I still believe the list presents a general overview that will suggest something of the variety and significance of the lands this book has been written to illuminate—the national lands, the inheritance shared by all Americans.

CHARLES S. WATSON, JR.

CALIFORNIA

King Range: Approximately 42 miles of northern California coastal grandeur (said to be more significant than the Pt. Reyes National Seashore), was established by Congress as the King Range National Conservation Area, under the administration of the Ukiah BLM District. For the first time in the BLM's history, authority was granted and $1.5 million appropriated for the BLM to purchase vital inholdings. The remarkable coastal portion of this area—often referred to as California's "Lost Coast"—will be set aside as a "recreation–primitive area complex," to protect a still largely de facto wilderness coastal landscape known to have many unique wild animals, birds, sea life, virgin Douglas fir, western red cedar, and oak forests.

Peninsular Range BLM Lands: Two major tracts of BLM lands, known as Otay Mountain and McCain Valley–InKoPah Ridge, are located near the Mexican border in San Diego County. The McCain–InKoPah tract is a remarkable desert-mountain transition zone reminiscent of the highlands of Baja California, with breathtaking views of the famed Anza–Borrego desert to the east. The Otay Mountain tract is but twenty-five miles from downtown San Diego, yet is one of the most remote and least explored regions in San Diego County. Only recently has it been revealed that the tract may have the only known occurrence of the rare Tecate cypress (*Supressus Guadalupensis*) in the United States.

Turtle Mountains: Recently declared a natural area by the Riverside BLM District, this remarkably pristine desert mountain area has many colorful and unique geological formations, including the rugged Mopah Peaks. The area also is a vital bighorn sheep area and has the farthest north native fan palms (*Washingtonia filifera*).

Whipple Mountains: Located near Parker Dam, in San Bernardino County, this area is a prime wilderness-natural area. Many persons, for instance, believe the famed saguaro cactus (*Carnegea gigantea*) occurs only in Arizona and Sonora, Mexico. Not so—California's only major stand of this largest of cacti species in the United States is found on BLM lands here.

Trona Pinnacles: Located near Searles Lake, this region of colorful volcanic pinnacles was deemed so significant that it has been designated a national natural landmark. The area includes many giant tufa formations (remnants of ancient geothermal springs which once lay beneath an ancient inland sea).

Dumont Dunes–Tecopa Bore: Located near Death Valley, this is one of the Mohave Desert's most unique sand-dune regions. Investigation is still under way to determine the extent of several unique plant types and persistent reports that the near-extinct Tecopa pupfish may still exist here. The area is regarded as the "key" in a classic conflict between conservationists who seek primitive area protection for such areas in the new Mohave Desert National Conservation Area, and off-road vehicle (ORV) enthusiasts, who want all public lands in the Mohave Desert kept open to unlimited ORV use. The Tecopa Bore, the suspected pupfish habitat area, is considered a prime ORV racecourse route. According to recent information developed by the Desert Fishes Council, the Tecopa Bore must still be regarded as a rare and endangered species habitat area.

Clark Mountain: Located near the Nevada line, this contains possibly the most diverse desert flora communities, including known occurrences of rare cacti and succulents, as well as a relict forest of virgin white fir. Considered one of the most scenic parts of the Mohave desert.

Yuha Basin: An area rich in paleontological, archeological, historical, and desert-flora qualities. One area, jointly administered by the BLM and the Imperial County Park Board, contains one of the purest stands of crucifixion thorn (*Holocantha emoryii*—not *Zzyphus jujuba*, the original Palestinian thorn bush famed in the crucifixion of Christ, as was suspected in 1968). The basin is also one of several major intaglio sites—figures of ancient primitive man origin formed over large areas in desert pavement and featured in the controversial movie, "Chariots of the Gods."

Eureka Dunes: One of the Bakersfield BLM District's outstanding trans-Sierra areas, located in Eureka Valley—a mountain range away from Death Valley. Occurring in this remarkable dune is a unique species of dune grass (*Ectosperma alerandre–Swall*), found nowhere else in the world. This site is a classic demonstration area for the need to reform present regulations that allow counties to build roads over public lands almost without restraint. In this area, road building by the Inyo County Department of Roads threatens this habitat area by creating easy ORV access.

Remnants of the "Redwood Empire": Many will be surprised to learn that the Ukiah BLM District—the same district charged with administration of the vital King Range—still has a least two known tracts of virgin redwoods (*Sequoia sempervirens*), one located in Mendocino County and the other in southern Humboldt County. The largest tract is reportedly nearly 100 acres of an undisturbed primeval stand. The smaller, in Humboldt County, was nearly destroyed by loggers who entered the area in trespass.

Lassen County Petroglyphs: Only recently has the Susanville BLM District discovered on its lands a twelve-mile canyon completely lined with a maze of petroglyphs, pictographs, and suspected intaglios. Its location is known only to a handful of government conservationists and to National Public Lands Task Force members, who have been sworn to secrecy concerning it.

Eagle Lake: A large Ice-Age remnant, this snow-fed lake is hemmed in by spectacular lava cliffs. In aeries and caves are found one of the last domains of the rare and endangered peregrine falcon and the near-extinct North American osprey. Located in the Susanville BLM District.

OREGON

The Steens Range: One of the world's most awe-inspiring Ice-Age marvels. An extended fault-block transverse ridge—with classic Sierra Nevada-type steep eastern escarpment—it contains possibly America's most distinctive U-shaped glacial-carved gorges. In addition to its volcanic wonders (such as the nearby Diamond Craters lava fields), the Steens Range is a wildlife treasure trove, with large herds of antelope and deer. Rich in archeology and history as well, it is a prime feature of the Burns BLM District. This range and its associated wonders became, in the late 1960s, the focal point for a pioneering Desert Trail movement (now organized as the Desert Trail Association) founded by environmentalist-educator Russell Pengelly of Burns, Oregon.

Owyhee River Canyons: Imperfectly mapped and possibly not fully explored, the Owyhee River uplands comprise millions of acres in extreme southeast Oregon, southwest Idaho, and north-central Nevada. The region is a series of high volcanic plains domed up and cut through by the Owyhee River and its numerous tributaries. The river flows 300 miles from the Humboldt Range in Nevada to the Snake River at Nyssa, receiving waters from Oregon's High Desert and Idaho's granitic Owyhee Mountains. The area contains deep, spectacular canyons, stretches of wild river, caves, natural arches and bridges, windows, and standing rock formations.

Trout Creek Mountains: Hard against the Oregon-Nevada border, in view of Steens Mountain and the Pine Forest Range, lie the Trout Creeks, a sub-alpine oasis in the High Desert. With elevations ranging between 5,000 and 8,000 feet in a 100,000-acre area, these block-fault mountains contain significant scenic, ecological, wildlife, geological, and paleontological values. There are cliffs, deep canyons, jagged ridges, alpine fell fields with clusters of lupine and phlox, hidden groves of aspen and mountain mahogany, pronghorn antelope, deer, elk, Indian relics, fossils, and outcroppings of old Mesozoic granodiorite. With forty inches of snow annually, streams persist throughout the year, and the Alvord Trout, found nowhere else in the world, makes its home in these.

Pueblo Mountains: The Pueblo Mountains, located south of Steens Mountain, include Pueblo Mountain (8725 ft.) and the Pueblo Mountain Range, which extends into Nevada. The mountains are characterized by big sagebrush and bunchgrass plant communities as well as volcanic rimrock outcroppings covered with colorful lichens. Numerous springs come off the ridges, permitting aspen and numerous herbs to thrive. Denio Creek and Van Horn Creek drain to the east through fairly steep canyons.

Fossil Mesozoic Peat Beds: Of all the wonders that have made the Oregon coast famous, one of the least known and most significant is this remarkable occurrence of a natural fossilized bog recently found on tidal flats and seashore lands administered by the Coos Bay BLM District. With vegetative matter so fresh, it is hard to believe this ancient peat bed has been fixed by geologists at 150 million years of age or older—which places it smack in the age of the dinosaurs. Experts consider this public-land find as significant as any fossil area yet identified. The nearby Coos Bay Wagon Road lands, administered by the Coos Bay BLM District, located in large scattered tracts in the heart of the Coast Range, contain extensive virgin forests—including unique groves of bay trees, called myrtlewood in Oregon, as well as live bogs with the rare "tiger lily" (*Darlingtonia californica*).

Cascade Foothills: Lying between the Forest Service-administered Cascade Range peaks and the broad Willamette Valley are extensive BLM public lands. Not the least of these are such "rain-forest" areas as the Wolf Creek Trail—a region of dense virgin forests, spectacular waterfalls, myriad wildlife and rare flora and Ice-Age glacial grooves. Recently, the Job Corps constructed an unusual rain-forest trail through a forest wonderland almost identical in appearance to such well known National Park phenomena as the Hoh Rain Forest of Olympic National Park in Washington. It is one of the chief attractions of the Roseburg BLM District.

Rogue River: The Rogue River—famed in the novels of Zane Grey—with its white water rapids and deep gorges cut through dark volcanic rock, is probably one of the best-known BLM wonders. It represents the earliest BLM program in the field of wild and scenic river preservation and is presently administered by the Medford BLM District. This district, along with neighboring Eugene and Coos Bay BLM Districts, administers one of the largest public-land forest regions outside Alaska. The best of these virgin Douglas fir and silver fir forests lies east of the Medford Valley, on checkerboarded public lands known as the Jackson-Klamath Master Units. Here are found giant fir trees known to exceed 500 years of age.

Deschutes River: Now one of Oregon's officially recognized systems of scenic and wild rivers, this deep-canyon river flows through a large tract of BLM lands for twenty-five miles—from Maupin through historic Sherar's Bridge to Mack Canyon, in the trans-Cascades near The Dalles. Famous as a fishing stream as well, the river winds and cuts through towering volcanic formations that are exceptionally colorful.

WASHINGTON

Chopaka Mountain: Although less than 300,000 acres of BLM lands remain in this state (administered by the Spokane BLM District), there are a number of significant BLM public land tracts—most notable of which is the spectacular Chopaka Mountain proposed primitive area, near Loomis, in the historic Okanogan Region. Lying adjacent to the Canadian border, this 5,000-acre public-land tract exhibits one of the most precipitous mountain slopes in the northern cascades—featuring a huge escarpment nearly 5,000 feet high. Nestled on the southern end of this slope is a huge fjordlike mountain lake—Chopaka Lake, lined with virgin alpine forests and a spectacular view of the Similkameen River far below.

"Z" Canyon: A noted deep canyonland—partially covered by BLM public lands—along the scenic Pend Oreille River in eastern Washington, "Z" Canyon is located near Metaline Falls and consists of a spectacular yellow-rock gorge—probably made up of highly weathered lavas and other volcanic rocks (such as rhyolite and andesite), through which flows the seasonally flooded river. The area is also noted, geologically, for extensive networks of caves.

ARIZONA

Gila Box: A prime primitive area and wild-river candidate, this is probably one of the least known and explored regions on eastern Arizona's
transitional Chihuahuan Desert public lands. This is the main canyon of
the upper Gila River, a few miles downriver from its Mogollon Rim head-
waters, in Graham and Greenlee counties. Administered by the Safford
BLM District, it is one of the grandest public-land canyons in the Southwest. The Gila Box is a geological treasure trove, with deep canyons,
jagged "hoodoos" (towering pinnacles of weathered volcanic rock),
geothermal springs, bat caves, and whitewater rapids. Although only
2,000 feet deep, it is nevertheless a breathtaking sight and gives the appearance of being much larger. More than any other public-land area in
Arizona, this region is typical of the Chihuahuan Deserts of southern New
Mexico and west Texas and has many cacti and succulent plant communities reminiscent of northeastern Mexico. From the canyon's south
rim to the Mexican border (including BLM lands in the nearby Peloncillo
and Chiricahua Mountains), there have been confirmed sightings of such
rare cats as the ocelot and jaguar (which are not found on any of Arizona's
typical Sonoran Deserts). Almost devoid of saguaros, the flora here is
marked by gardens of ocotillo, sotol, and beavertail cactus. In this Gila
River region is found the rare Gila trout (*Salmo gilae*) and the Gila Top-
minnow (*Poeciliopsis occidentalis*).

Aravaipa Canyon: One of the BLM's first primitive areas, set aside by
proclamation in January 1969, and one of Arizona's best preserved Sonoran Desert canyons, it includes a fourteen-mile section of Aravaipa Creek
as it passes through the rugged Pinaleno and Galiuro Mountains in eastern Pinal County. A picturesque stream, this section of Aravaipa Creek
consists of vertical canyon walls, mysterious side canyons, forests of giant
saguaro, and such wildlife as deer, javelina, and cougar. The river contains at least seven species of rare and endangered fish—the Gila sucker
(*Pantosteus clarki*), Sonora sucker (*Catostomus insignis*), western speck-
led dace (*Rhinichthys osculus*), loach minnow (*Tiaroga cobitis*), longfin
dace (*Agosia chrysogaster*), roundtail chub (*Gila robusta*) and spike dace
(*Meda fulgida*). Aravaipa Canyon also is a unique U.S. habitat of the rare
Mexican long-eared bat (*Plecotus phyllotus*).

Paria Canyon: The second of the BLM's early primitive areas, set aside by
President Lyndon Johnson in January 1969, encompasses forty-five miles
of the sublime canyons of the Paria River in northern Arizona and southern Utah's windswept Colorado Plateau. Buffering the area is the
50,135-acre Vermillion Cliffs Natural Area, a region of towering red and
orange sandstone cliffs overlooking the rugged, narrow Marble Gorge of
the Colorado River. Located between Lee's Ferry (in Arizona) and High-
way 89 bridge east of Kanab (in Utah), Paria Canyon Primitive Area is a
fantastic maze of deep, winding sandstone canyons—with sheer vertical

walls plunging between 1,500 and 2,000 feet. The most unique feature is an almost exact "mirror image" replica of Rainbow Bridge. This natural bridge guards the mouth of a side canyon—Wrather Canyon—and lies in the deepest part of Paria Canyon. The canyon also boasts huge amphitheaters of overhanging sandstone rock, weird formations, artifacts, petroglyphs, pictographs, historic Mormon pioneer sites, and pristine springs.

The Fred J. Weiler Memorial "Greenbelt": Fred J. Weiler was BLM State director for Arizona from 1961 to 1970. Weiler died while on a safari in Kenya, but in his lifetime he became almost a legend in the Bureau, leading the effort to establish new wilderness and wildlife-management programs on our BLM public lands. His untimely death robbed us of a prime public-land environmentalist—and in his memory, the Arizona BLM recently designated this "Greenbelt" (a Class III "natural environment area") encompassing all of those public lands lying adjacent to the lower Gila River. The Greenbelt covers a distance of 100 miles, between Buckeye (in Maricopa County) to Date Palm (in Yuma County). Hopefully to be included in primitive-area status are the cactus gardens of the rugged Gila Bend Mountains north of the river.

The "Arizona Strip": A vast region of high plains bordering the north rim of the spectacular Toroweap Narrows of the Grand Canyon (formerly the area in the Grand Canyon National Monument), this is a sprawling area that represents one of the few remnants of America's "last frontier." There are occasional rugged mountains—such as the remote Virgin Mountains (now undergoing hearings toward establishment as a 32,000-acre BLM Primitive Area). Cutting the edges of this broad *altiplano* are equally spectacular smaller canyons, such as Hacks Canyon and Kanab Canyon (both potential Primitive Areas). It is one of the BLM's most significant wildlife regions—including antelope, bighorn sheep, wild turkey, mule deer, Gambel quail, and several aeries of our nation's symbol, the bald eagle.

Hualapai—Music Mountains: Perhaps northwest Arizona's most rugged landscapes, with remote peaks rising over 8,400 feet, this area lies in a profound biological transition zone—featuring the Joshua tree forests of the Mohave Desert and the tall saguaros of the Sonoran desert. In this area and in the nearby gorges and hills of Burro Creek and the Big Sandy, the two desert types meet.

NEVADA

Red Rock Canyon: A majestic, pristine desert paradise only 20 miles from the Las Vegas Strip. In 1968, after a NORA select study committee perused the area in the early 1960s (and submitted the first citizens' study to the Las Vegas BLM District in April 1964), a BLM team headed by recreation chief Eldon F. Holmes successfully implemented a plan leading to the establishment of this first BLM "recreation-natural area complex" (now known as "recreation lands"). Red Rock has at least thirty-three floral types that are considered rare, endangered, or unique to the Great Basin. It is one of two places in Nevada where the rare Gila monster has been sighted. Its rugged sandstone cliffs support forests of virgin ponderosa, piñon, Joshua trees, and ancient bristlecone pines. If based on archeology alone, Red Rock would still be of great significance—with its myriad petroglyphs, pictographs (with original pigment remarkably well preserved), and ceremonial sites. Including 63,000 acres, Red Rock is considered the cornerstone of a future BLM system.

Leviathan Cave: Discovered in 1963 during a NORA field expedition headed by noted spelunker Alvin McLane of Reno, after a U.S. Geological Survey aerial photograph showed what appeared to be a gaping hole in a remote eastern Nevada mountain range. The hole was a 180-foot by 100-foot "picture-window" entrance to a huge cavern containing remarkable cave speliothems. The cave—300 feet high and 800 feet long—was created eons ago when a huge interior mass of the mountain collapsed, leaving this immense room. A later NORA expedition also discovered a forest of ancient bristlecone pines (*Pinus longaeva*, still recognized as the world's oldest living thing) on the slopes above the cave. In 1969 the cave and its immediate environs were classified as a Bureau of Outdoor Recreation Class IV area (natural area) and to protect it, its precise location has since been kept a closely guarded secret.

High Rock Canyon: Located in extreme northwest Nevada, this Susanville BLM District area actually is a system of five spectacular canyons carved by wind, ice, and water erosion from a sprawling lava plateau. In 1846 pioneer trailblazers Jesse and Lindsay Applegate discovered it while seeking a shortcut off the California Trail to southern Oregon. Later, parties were escorted through by such pioneers as Peter Lassen. In the early 1850s, wagon trains passed through—leaving several sets of unique axlegrease and carved inscriptions on the towering canyon walls (lower High Rock Canyon). Numerous springs were found, in addition to the inscriptions, by a 1961 NORA expedition; these springs may contain the rare and endangered desert dace (previously only known to occur at Soldier Meadows, to the east of High Rock Canyon area). Upper High Rock Canyon once contained an extensive virgin great Basin wild-rye meadow, which has since suffered greatly from mismanaged grazing.

Blue Lake: Following a tip given it by a Basque sheepherder in 1959, NORA eventually led several expeditions to this incredible alpine wonder on BLM lands (Winnemucca BLM District) on the northern edge of the great Black Rock desert. Set high in a remote mountain range, this Ice-Age remnant glacial lake lies in a grand amphitheaterlike cirque—surrounded by rugged peaks, breathtaking vistas, virgin forests (whitebark pines, and along the southernmost limits of its range, limber pines and aspen), and such wildlife as the golden eagle, bald eagle, peregrine falcon, mountain lion, deer, and pronghorn antelope. A 27,000-acre primitive area has been recommended by the Winnemucca BLM District (conservationists want 40,000 acres), consisting of two units, which in mid-1974 ran into heated political opposition from diehard miners and local cattlemen. In spite of this, the BLM has made a decision in favor of primitive-area and natural-area status for the two units, at the reduced acreage.

"Rock of Ages"-South Schell Creek Range Botanical Area: In May 1966, this hitherto unknown bristlecone pine (*Pinus longaeva*) area was discovered. What makes this find remarkable are the low elevations at which this species is found, its association with Sonoran-desert cacti and plants, and its vigorous growths (it is one of few places where youthful regeneration is still very active). The region has several scattered forests of bristlecone, mainly on the exposed western slopes, set in a limestone alpine ridge. Located in the Ely BLM District, straddling the Lincoln-White Pine County line, it includes 15,000 acres.

Morey Peak: This rugged 10,000-foot central Nevada peak is a truly remarkable find, with towering peaks resembling the Swiss Alps and no less than three separate sets of desert-bound waterfalls, one with a tumbling cataract over 1,000 feet high. It also includes an ancient forest of bristlecone pines, the only known occurrence in volcanic rock in Nevada (indeed, this may be the *only* occurrence of this species of bristlecone pine—*Pinus longaeva*—to be found in such an environment). In addition, the approaches to this mountain massif are rife with intricate petroglyphs and carvings of primitive man, perhaps 10,000 to 15,000 years old.

North Black Rock Desert Natural Area (proposed): Located on a sprawling northerly extension of the vast Black Rock Desert in northern Nevada (Humboldt and Pershing counties in the Winnemucca BLM District), this is one of the largest relatively untouched tracts of forbidding Lahontan-Ice-Age landscapes. Alkali flats, extending like giant fingers around half-buried Great Basin ranges and lava fields, extend more than 100 uninterrupted miles. Along the fringes of one of these desert "fingers" is a remarkable region of steaming geothermal springs, ancient primitive-man campsites, remnants of the historic Applegate Cutoff Trail (1846–54), and strange geological formations. One of the springs, known as Double Hot Springs, consists of two lens-shaped hot springs which apparently arrived at this desert surface, almost touching each other, from apparently separate deep-seated magma chambers. Nearby are historic ruins along the Applegate Trail (where the trail ruts may still be seen), known as "Hardin City," which is believed to be the site where the noted trailblazer Peter Lassen was murdered by unknown assailants.

The Fort Mohave Tract: In Nevada's southernmost tip lies the state's only region of lower Colorado River desert riparian bottomlands. Here, Nevada has 9,000 acres still administered by the BLM—and it is one of only three such areas along the lower Colorado River between Las Vegas and Yuma. At first sight it appears to be a drab piece of river floodplain; biological wonders usually come in well-disguised forms. Yet recent investigations have shown this tract to be priceless indeed. It has Nevada's only undisturbed groves of "smoke trees" (*Dalea spinosa*), possibly the state's only natural occurrence, as well as ocotillo (also rare in Nevada). Wildlife is this tract's real bounty, with known sightings of the endangered Gila monster, desert tortoise, and Yuma clapper rail. In 1961 Nevada forced passage of the Fort Mohave Act, which gave the state a ten-year option to select this land. After the ten-year period had passed, Nevada's Colorado River Commission, in the words of a BLM official, had failed "to find a sucker who'd take it off their hands." After the expiration, Nevada gamblers and developers saw the marina-condominium-Disneyland-gambling-spa potential of the tract, and convinced the commission to renew efforts to acquire it from the BLM. Secretary Rogers Morton, without any congressional mandate, arrived at a "gentleman's agreement" with CRC officials to extend the provisions of the Fort Mohave Act beyond its 1971 expiration date, a move that faces possible legal challenge by conservationists.

Tule Ridge–Incandescent Rocks Primitive Area (proposed): North of Sparks, in central Washoe County, is another of Nevada's little-known Great Basin ranges deemed to have prime wilderness potential. Consisting largely of intrusive basalts and lavas, this mountain range has, over eons of time, gouged and carved a system of strange, red-rock pinnacles and narrow defiles which at certain times of the day exhibit a remarkable luminescence (identical to that noted at famed Ayres Rock in the Australian outback). The area has a high priority among potential primitive areas being considered by the Carson City BLM District. Incandescent Rocks is just one of nearly 100 potential primitive areas, natural and scenic areas, and wild-river areas in Nevada alone.

IDAHO

The Owyhee Desert: One of the first areas to be investigated by NORA's national organization—the National Public Lands Task Force (created in 1967). Located in southwestern Idaho, generally lying south of the Snake River, it is easily the most mysterious and scenic desert region in the state. It is represented by spectacular canyons of such Snake River tributaries as the Bruneau and Owyhee (a derivation of the word "Hawaiian") rivers. It is also a region of sublime waterfalls (Jump River Canyon), geothermal springs ("Indian Bathtub," near Bruneau Canyon), geological phenomena ("balanced rock" near Castleford, in Salmon Falls Canyon) and huge sand dunes (Eagle Cove Sand Hills), as well as being one of the most significant pronghorn antelope rangelands in the Pacific Northwest.

The Snake River Plain: When Sir Arthur Conan Doyle penned his "Lost World," he must have envisaged this land. Consisting of millions of acres of BLM lands in south-central Idaho (near Arco and Twin Falls), it is essentially the best of two kinds of country—a sprawling surface of recent, violent volcanism and an eerie subterranean world of largely unknown rivers, springs, and caves. Even today, little of it is known and there are parts allegedly never seen by man. The jagged lava fields are very similar to the famed Craters of the Moon (indeed, the present national monument comprises only a tiny portion of this vast area). Near Arco, one of the area's more unique features is a grey limestone natural bridge (its location, like Leviathan Cave in Nevada, is a well-kept secret).

Mineral Ridge Scenic Area: Not much BLM public land remains in northern Idaho, except a few scattered tracts of a few hundred acres to a section or more in size. One of these, however, lies along the north shore of Coeur D'Alene Lake. Here the Spokane BLM District has established a small scenic preserve including a portion of Beauty Bay (an arm of Coeur D'Alene Lake) and a rugged woodland covering a portion of the geologically important Idaho batholith (a granitic intrusion) which is associated with other rocks of pre-Cambrian age (roughly 600 million to 1 billion years old).

NEW MEXICO

The Chihuahuan Desert: Only a small part of the American Southwest is represented by this desert, which covers most of northeastern Mexico and the Sierra Oriental. It is characterized by flora, wildlife, and climatic conditions quite different from the more predominant (in the U.S.) Sonoran Desert to the west. Most of the last remaining Chihuahuan desert wildlands in the U.S. are found on public lands of the Gadsden Purchase of 1848 and largely restricted to the south-central and southwestern counties of Doña Ana, Luna, and Hidalgo (Las Cruces BLM District). Here the land is characterized by massive lava flows, rocky limestone crags, gardens of cacti, succulents, and tree-yuccas, and such wildlife as bighorn sheep, javelina, mule deer, Coues white-tailed deer, and antelope. On the higher slopes (such as the 97,920-acre Big Hatchet Mountain Wildlife Area) one sees a landscape truly representative of the Mexican cordilleran ranges, with forests of live oak, alligator juniper, desert willow, and hackberry.

Fort Stanton–Pecos River Lands: This region is largely administered by the Roswell BLM District and is well noted as an outstanding region for caves. There may be thousands of them, 200 of which are now under investigation. One cave, on a 27,000-acre tract in BLM jurisdiction (Fort Stanton tract), was revealed to have possibly seven miles of tunnels and subterranean rooms—filled with marvelous speliothems and relics of primeval man. In addition, such strange wildlife as the rare jaguarundi (native to Mexico and Central America) have been reported in canyons of the Pecos River.

Rio Grande Gorge: Near Taos in northern New Mexico, where the historic Rio Grande meets the Red River, the BLM still holds lands encompassing seventy miles of spectacular weathered cliffs and canyons. Much of the river and its deep chasm is now part of this nation's wild-river system. For thousands of years the river carved its defile out of highly resistant volcanic rock—tempered over the centuries with forests of juniper, piñon, grasslands, and fields of wildflowers. In the river are trout and other game fish—while the canyon's heights remain the domain of bobcats, cougar, bald and golden eagles. To the west, along the Continental Divide, the BLM administers a vast region of badlands and portions of the famed Painted Desert with whole valleys filled with thousands of balanced rocks, toadstools, and the fossil remains of dinosaurs and petrified wood.

COLORADO—UTAH

Canyonlands: Of nowhere in the West can it truly be said that as much of the American frontier remains intact as it does here—from the escarpments of the Kaiparowitz, the San Rafael Swell, and the Roan-Beckwith-Book Cliffs through magnificent canyons carved by the Green, San Juan, Colorado, Dolores, and Escalante rivers, as well as the Grand Gulch, Hatch, and Dirty Devil Washes. In the Monticello BLM District alone there are probably at least 2,000 cliff dwellings and ancient pueblo ruins. In the Henry Mountains (Richfield BLM District) roam one of the last of America's truly wild bison herds. In the canyon of the Dolores River one can see nearly all the famed Grand Canyon geological sequences. Deeply etched into the land are such remote little-known canyons as Dark Canyon, Red Canyon, and Moki Canyon, and such weird geological phenomena as the Waterpocket Fold and the Valley of the Gods. Not all the great canyons of the Green and the Colorado have been transferred to the National Park Service—Desolation Canyon (Price BLM District), famed for its adventurous rapids, and large portions of the canyons of the San Juan River remain a part of the public lands. In Colorado a huge tectonic uplift of the Uncompahgre Plateau—consuming eons of time—having diverted such major rivers as the Colorado and the Gunnison and left exposures of white, red, pink, and orange sandstone formations of every size, shape, and description. In southern Colorado's San Juan Mountains, the BLM retains jurisdiction over a region of 14,000-foot Rocky Mountain peaks (Lake Fork lands, Montrose BLM District, including the newly established 40,400-acre Powderhorn Primitive Area). Indeed, much of the sublime beauty seen by Major Powell's historic 1869 expedition is still there, just as glorious now as it was then. Yet—lacking a formal Organic Act to preserve such wonders—the various BLM districts in the canyonlands are under tremendous pressure to open up these lands to coal and oil-shale strip mining and even to provide additional lands for coal-fuel plants.

Escalante Canyons Outstanding Natural Area: While most of the magnificent Escalante Canyons system is now part of the Glen Canyon National Recreation Area, all of this beautiful canyon system upstream from Harris Wash remains under BLM jurisdiction. This section of the river extends downstream from Calf Creek to the GCNRA boundary, and it contains perhaps the most beautiful section of the main canyon. Tributaries include Boulder Creek, Deer Creek, The Gulch, Horse Canyon, Phipps Canyon, and Bowington Arch Canyon. The area is rich in archeological treasures, natural arches, and flower-strewn benches.

Phipps–Death Hollow Outstanding Natural Area: This section of the Escalante River drainage includes the river from Escalante town downstream to Calf Creek. It includes two of the Escalante's most delicate and beautiful tributary streams, Death Hollow (Mamie Creek) and Sand Wash. The Death Hollow system is a deep, narrow canyon unique in that it has never been grazed by cattle and depends only on springs for its permanent flow. The main canyon here contains one of the best preserved Anasazi ruins in the area, and there are rare pictographs associated.

Canaan Mountain: This is a high, rugged escarpment directly south of Zion Canyon National Park, and rising vertically from the Rockville, Utah, city limits. It is a huge block of Navajo sandstone, and in many ways it is the equal of Zion. Its summit is a rugged plateau of almost incomparable beauty, and its vertical sides have left it inaccessible and virtually undisturbed by man. It is currently closed to ORV's, and is proposed for primitive area status by the Kanab District Office of the BLM.

Hondu: This little-visited area lies along the south ridge of the San Rafael Swell. Named for a huge natural arch and butte within the area, the region includes the spectacular canyon system of the Muddy River. One of the deepest and narrowest canyons of the region, its high walls, beautiful benches, and forbidding appearance have discouraged all but a few from savoring its solitude. The region is being proposed as a primitive area by the Richfield District of the BLM.

Little Rockies: Geologically a part of the Henry Mountain chain, the Little Rockies form the two southernmost peaks of the last mountain range to be discovered and named in the continental United States. Adjacent to the Glen Canyon National Recreation Area not far south of Hite, the area comprises some of the best remaining habitat of the now-rare Desert Bighorn Sheep. It is being proposed for primitive area status by the Richfield District of the BLM.

Sid's Mountain, Mexican Mountain, Heve's Canyon, Keesle Country:
These areas comprise the best and most rugged areas of the San Rafael
Swell north of the Muddy River. This huge upwarp of sandstone domi-
nates the landscape for mile around, and contains some of eastern Utah's
best potential wilderness. While much of this country has been dug and
blasted for its potential uranium deposits, its deeply dissected surface
prevented its total exploitation, and much of it today remains undisturbed.

Wah Wah Mountains: This desolate, dry, and steep range in Utah's west
desert country has been almost ignored by almost everybody, including
Indians, pioneers, and exploiters. When the U.S. Geological Survey went
through in the late fifties they found its ridges sprinkled with some of the
finest and oldest specimens of the rare bristlecone pine known. The area
is being proposed as a primitive area by the Filmore District of the BLM.

Robber's Roost—Dirty Devil: The Dirty Devil begins at Hanksville, Utah, as
a fusion of the Fremont River and the Muddy River. From here it flows
south and east into what used to be the Colorado River just above Hite.
The main canyon is not as spectacular as the Escalante, but it has beautiful
walls in spots and some magnificent tributaries in the Robber's Roost
Canyon system. This area was the hideout and staging area for Utah's
most celebrated outlaw gang, the Wild Bunch (Butch Cassidy and the
Sundance Kid).

Fifty Mile Mountain: Also called the Straight Cliffs, this region comprises
the northernmost limits of the Kaiparowits Plateau. It rises directly from
the desert south of the Escalante River, and is three-quarters of a mile
above Lake Powell. Its surface is a long unexcavated archeological site,
and the views of Utah's canyon country from its rims are unexcelled.

Beef Basin: If you want to see the best collection of Indian ruins in Utah,
Beef Basin is the place to go. The whole area lies directly south of Canyonlands National Park, and is an archeological treasure house. Most of the
ruins lie on the flat, juniper-covered desert, and are largely unprotected.
The area is criss-crossed by roads of varying quality, and will be difficult
to save.

WYOMING

Red Desert: If one had to call to mind the Western state where conservationists had the least success achieving wilderness, natural-area, and
wild-river preservation, it would be Wyoming. Stockmen have controlled
the BLM districts here with an iron fist, and yet there are areas that can
still be saved. Most notable of these is the immense southwestern expanse
known as the Red Desert, which is reputed to be the finest pronghorn

antelope range in America. Bordering this huge, windswept *altiplano* are rugged Rocky Mountain summits, such as Green Mountain and Ferris Mountain, with virgin forests of pine, clear streams with native fish, and such wildlife as deer, antelope, elk, and moose. There is little doubt of the primeval, de facto wilderness condition of several public-land tracts within this region—so vast that it lies within three BLM districts: Rawlins, Rock Springs, and Lander-Pinedale—yet the Wyoming BLM State Office has so far announced not a single firm primitive area/wild river proposal for any of the public lands of this state. Archeologically and historically this region is especially significant, with its well-preserved remnants of the Oregon Trail (several places where wheel ruts can still be seen), early forts, gravesites, ghost towns, pioneer inscriptions, and artifacts of primitive man. It is generally believed, in spite of rampant overgrazing, that there are many areas with virgin prairie grasslands largely intact. It also is believed that these native prairies may have rare and endangered species of plants and vital forage—in addition to "booming" grounds for prairie chickens and sage grouse.

MONTANA

Missouri River: If Lewis and Clark were somehow able to return and visit the remaining public lands adjacent to this great American riverway, they would find them little changed. It is incredible to note, in the Space Age, that there remain extensive primeval conditions—in the form of native grasslands, Rocky Mountain bighorn sheep habitats, untrammeled canyonlands, and untamed rapids—along one of our nation's largest rivers. While the once majestic bison are gone, such wildlife as the elk, moose, bear, antelope, prairie chicken, and wild turkey remain. Indeed, in these historic and still wild waters are such strange and unique fish as the shovel-nosed sturgeon (*Acipenser transmontanous*), Arctic grayling (in the upper portions of tributaries, now a rarity in the river itself), and the bizarre, primitive anachronism of this river—the paddlefish (*Polyodon spathula*).

The Centennial Range: A prime candidate for primitive area status, this region crosses the Idaho-Montana line in the Dillon BLM District in southwestern Montana. Here, jagged peaks with perennial snows and virgin forests of aspen, whitebark pine, and Douglas fir range to altitudes just under 10,000 feet. The range guards the southern approaches to one of America's most important migratory wildlife areas—Red Rock Lakes. Having much of the Rocky Mountain majesty of nearby Yellowstone National Park, the BLM's Centennial Range shares one of America's great geographic features—the Continental Divide.

Humbug Spires—Bear Trap Canyon: Also located in the Dillon BLM District, these two areas were set aside as BLM primitive areas in 1972 by

Interior Secretary Rogers Morton. Humbug Spires, near Butte, consisting of 7,041 acres, is a region of ponderosa-clad hills studded with hundreds of stark, white granite spires. They are part of a large igneous intrusion known to geologists as a "batholith," resulting in the awesome monoliths found in this administrative BLM preserve. The smallest of the BLM's national system of primitive areas is 3,639-acre Bear Trap Canyon, near Norris, in Madison County. Bear Trap Canyon is a finely chiseled 1,500-foot-deep chasm cut through the Madison Range by one of the main sources of the Missouri, the Madison River. Biologically, it is a transition zone, with flora of the Rocky Mountains merging with those of the Great Plains. It is remarkably similar to another spectacular gorge, along the Missouri itself, known as Hauser Narrows—which still awaits formal designation by the Missoula BLM District.

PICTURE CREDITS

Bruce Barnbaum. Page 167, top: Denver Public Library, Western Collection. Pages 167, bottom, 172–173, 177: Bureau of Land Management. Page 179, top: Charlie Ott; bottom: William E. Keyes. Page 182: Bruce Barnbaum. Pages 184–185: Bureau of Land Management. Page 188: Los Angeles County Museum of Natural History, History Division. Page 191: Bureau of Land Management. Page 194: Susan Landor. Page 198: David Plowden. Page 203, top: Daniel Gridley; bottom: World Book Science Service. Page 205: Bureau of Land Management. Page 208: Denver Public Library, Western Collection. Page 213: Ed Cooper. Page 217, top: Bureau of Land Management; bottom: David Meunch. Page 220: Ed Cooper.

ACKNOWLEDGMENTS

The authors wish to thank the following individuals for their help in preparing this book: Roger Olmsted, former editor of the *Sierra Club Bulletin*, who first recognized the value of such a book and brought the authors together; Wallace Stegner, who read the book in manuscript and gave his enthusiasm to the project; Robert Wazeka, the Sierra Club's Oregon Coordinator, who also read the book in manuscript as well as contributed to the completion of the "Wilderness Index"; Daniel Gridley, of the *Bulletin* staff, who collected most of the BLM photographs and opened his own extensive picture files to us; and Patricia Kollings, editor of The American West Publishing Company, who made many historical pictures available. No one mentioned here, of course, should be held responsible for any errors of fact or interpretation which this book may contain; these are the sole and exclusive property of the authors.